THE BOOK OF

COMING FORTH BY DAY

The Ethics of the Declarations of Innocence

Also by the Author

Essays on Struggle: Position and Analysis

The Foundations of Kawaida Theory

Introduction to Black Studies

Kawaida Theory: An Introductory Outline

Selections From The Husia:
Sacred Wisdom of Ancient Egypt

The African American Holiday of Kwanzaa:
A Celebration of Family, Community
and Culture

THE BOOK OF

COMING FORTH BY DAY

The Ethics of the Declarations of Innocence

Translation and Commentary

MAULANA KARENGA

University of Sankore Press

Los Angeles, California

Cover: The scribe Ani and his wife, Tutu, in the Great Hall of Judgement.

Typesetting: Tiamoyo Karenga

First Printing: 1990

THE BOOK OF COMING FORTH BY DAY: The Ethics of the Declarations of Innocence.

ISBN 0-943412-14-5

To the men and women of Us Organization, and their research arm, the Institute of Pan-African Studies, the unannounced yet very deserving workers and soldiers on the battlefield of African culture who saw the need for a formal structure to study and restore African classical culture and to harness the intellectual and practical energies of those interested and involved, and who made the first moves to build it.

Homage to them, then, who planned, called and financed the founding conference of the Association for the study of Classical African Civilizations (ASCAC), who gave the Association its name, its logo, its conference format and its first literature, and, who have produced the bulk of its literature and a cadre of _Seba_, moral teachers in the tradition of ancient Egypt, to teach that literature and the culture which produced it.

Contents

Contents

Preface

This volume is another contribution to two ongoing projects - one, general, the other specific. First, it is another contribution to the general ongoing historical project of rescuing and reconstructing African culture which is at the heart of the mission of two organizations of which I am a founding member - Us Organization and the Association for the Study of Classical African Civilizations (ASCAC). In 1965, Us contended that the key crisis and challenge in African life was one of culture, the challenge to rescue and reconstruct the best of ancient African culture and use it as a paradigm for a renewed modern African culture and community. Only then, Us argued, could African people retake control of their destiny and daily lives, shape their world in their own image and interest and step back on the stage of human history as a free, proud and productive people. Also, only in this way could they speak their own special truth to the world and make their own unique contribution to the forward flow of human history.

In 1980 I taught a seminar on classical African civilization at the Institute of Pan-African Studies, the research arm of Us. Using material from my book, <u>Introduction to Black Studies</u> (1) which was published in 1982 and has become the standard introductory text in the field, I began to raise questions about the essentiality of classical civilization in the restoration project. It is in this context that Us began to discuss the relevance of ancient Egypt (Kemet) and the practical implications of using it as a paradigm for the rescue and reconstruction of African culture. In 1981 we initiated these conversations around Cheikh Anta Diop's works on ancient

Egypt and the functions he assigned it in the overall project of African cultural restoration.

Diop argued cogently, and we of Us came to agree, that ancient Egypt was the key classical African civilization given its abundance of documents, its level of achievement in various areas of culture and human knowledge and its resultant significance to other African cultures as well as to world culture. It was his contention that until we rescued and reconstructed ancient Egyptian history we would always appear as debtors to the world rather than vice versa which is the historical truth. Moreover, he saw three basic functions for ancient Egypt as a cultural paradigm for the restoration of Africa as a continent and world community. Serving the central role that Graeco-Roman civilization serves for Europe, a rescued Egypt, he maintained could be used to "reconcile African civilization with history, build a body of modern human sciences and renew African culture" (2).

The first function is to set the historical record straight concerning the African contribution to human civilization and history and to demonstrate the debt the world, especially Europe, owes Africa thru Egypt. The second and third functions are to provide a paradigm of cultural thought and practice which not only lays the basis for a new approach to and insight into the human sciences, but also lays the basis for the reinvigoration and expansion of African culture. In a word, it will provide an indispensible foundation on which to raise our cultural future as African peoples and as a world historical community.

Accepting this contention and line of reasoning after due deliberation, Us and its research arm, the Institute of Pan-African Studies, decided it was time to assemble the various strands in the academic, political and cultural movement community who were somehow involved in the study of ancient Egypt and committed to its restoration as a cultural paradigm. This led to a series of contacts and conversations with people in the field, especially with Dr. Jacob Carruthers to whom we extended an invitation to join us in holding the First Annual Ancient Egyptian Studies Conference in February 1984 in Los Angeles. It is in these conversations and those at the Conference that the basic outlines of ASCAC were formulated and discussed and at our next meeting in Chicago, they were consolidated and reaffirmed.

It is in the context of our work in ASCAC that this volume represents another more specific contribution. For it is another contribution to the specific project of rescuing and reconstructing the literature of Kemet, especially its ethical literature and using it not only as a guide to a moral, meaningful and truly human life, but also to engage in modern ethical discourse from an African worldview. This project which began in Us in 1983 and carried over in ASCAC was advanced with the publication in 1984 for the Conference of my Selections From The Husia: Sacred Wisdom of Ancient Egypt (3). As the title suggested, this was just selections from a planned larger work, the Husia. When finished, this work will include the major sacred literature of ancient Egypt with emphasis on ethics and serve as an African sacred text many had called for, but could not produce for various reasons.

The Husia, then, is an ongoing project and this translation of and commentary on Chapter 125 of the Book of Coming Forth By Day with emphasis on the ethics of the Declarations of Innocence is a contribution to this project. This volume is also a reflection of my commitment to the recommendations I made in 1986, as chair of the Spiritual Commission of ASCAC, concerning the need to continually project Kemetic literature and share it with the masses of African people.

Our organization, Us, has always stressed the importance of studying the original literature of the ancient Egyptians themselves as opposed to secondary sources which vary from racist to occultist - and in any case problematic - interpretations of the Kemetic texts. Our position has been and remains that one cannot truly know Kemet without studying its literature. For its religion, ethics, culture, science, politics are in its literature. And thus, one will remain pathetically dependent on others to interpret one's culture if one does not master the literature him/herself. It is important at this point to note that at one level one need not know Medu Netcher, the language of ancient Egypt, itself, to know the literature. For believers of other traditions may or may not read the original language of their sacred texts. But they study the texts even in translations and count on committed scholars to do reliable translations and critical exegeses of the texts.

This volume, then, is, above all, another contribution to the Husitic project begun in 1983 and reaffirmed in my ASCAC Spiritual Commission report of 1986. It is a project which has four basic aims: (1) to make available the literature of Kemet thru translation and publication; 2) to discuss the literature in writings, classes, seminars, lectures, conferences, etc.; 3) to train Seba, moral teachers in the ancient Egyptian tradition, to study systematically and thoroughly and to teach the literature with clarity, incisiveness and commitment, and finally; (4) to integrate it into our daily lives so that practice of its principles may enrich and expand our lives and contribute to the posing and bringing into being a new African and truly human society.

The Institute of Pan-African Studies has committed itself to this project and is pursuing it on all four levels. Thus, we publish Kemetic literature and commentary on it. We also teach it in the various contextes and forms cited above. And we have for six years trained a group of Seba, or moral teachers in the Maatian tradition of ancient Egypt, who in turn assist groups and persons across the country in the integration of Maatian ethical philosophy and principles in their daily lives.

In conclusion, let me give thanks to all those who have made my work possible, enjoyable and challenging. First, I extend ongoing gratitude to the members of Us and the Institute of Pan-African Studies to whom I have dedicated this work. It is in this communitarian African context that my vision, values and practice evolve and are sustained. Also, I give thanks to the Sebati, and the Seba, who have studied and sacrificed to grasp and grow within the ethical legacy of Kemetic culture; to Tiamoyo Karenga, my friend, co-worker and companion in all things good and beautiful; to Chimbuko Tembo and Limbiko Tembo, my publishers and special friends; to Jitahadi Imara and Subira Kifano, my vice-chairs in Us, my assistant directors at the Institute of Pan-African Studies, and my colleagues in work and struggle; and to all of those who in the midst of it all have called, written or in passing stopped to say thanks for doing an important work - for us and history.

Maulana Karenga
Institute of Pan-African Studies
Los Angeles, California

March, 1990 (6230 A.F.E.)

Notes

1. Maulana Karenga. Introduction to Black Studies, Los Angeles, CA: University of Sankore Press, 1982.

2. Cheikh Anta Diop. Civilisation ou Barbarie, Paris: Presence Africaine, 1981, p. 12.

3. Maulana Karenga. Selections from the Husia: Sacred Wisdom of Ancient Egypt, Los Angeles: CA: University of Sankore Press, 1984.

SECTION I - INTRODUCTION

Chapter I

INTRODUCTION

I. Historical Background

Certainly, the most well-known ancient Egyptian sacred text is The Book of Coming Forth By Day. It is usually called the Book of the Dead, a name reportedly given to it by the German Egyptologist, Richard Lepsius, and other egyptologists who obtained copies of it from Egyptian peasants who stated they had found it buried with the dead. The correct name of the book, however, is given in its first chapter as "Rw Prt M Hrw" or Ru Pert em Heru" - The Book of Coming Forth by Day (1). Actually, the word "rw" means chapters, sayings or utterances, but it has come to mean through consensus and usage "book" in this case. In other cases, book is either medjat, tchau or shefedu, and in a more general sense of something written - shes. Moreover, "pert" may mean "going forth" or "coming forth". In fact, Thomas G. Allen (2) translates it as "going forth", while others like Miriam Lichtheim, R.O. Faulkner and E.A. Wallis Budge translate it as "coming forth". In any case, it refers to a process which involves breaking the bonds of death and grave and coming forth to bask in sunlight in a spiritual sense. It is both a vision and aspiration to overcome death, to go and come freely in heaven and earth and assume any form in any place one's spirit wishes to be [3].

The geneology of the Book of Coming Forth by Day begins with the so-called Pyramid Texts or what we have called the Book of Rising and Transformation [4]. It was a custom to place sacred texts in the tombs of the departed as early as the Old Kingdom. In fact, in the Fifth Dynasty, [ca. 2400-2300 B.C.E.], King Unas, the last king of the dynasty, adorned the interior walls of his pyramid at Saqqara with sacred texts. This began a practice which subsequent kings of the Sixth Dynasty [ca. 2300-2150 B.C.E.] followed. It is in these texts that the ideas of rising and transformation, immortality, and ethical justification, which we find later in the Book of Coming Forth by Day, first appear.

With the collapse of central authority during the First Intermediate Period [ca. 2135-2040 B.C.E.], we find an expansion of the use of these sacred texts. Whereas these texts were once essentially used by royalty, persons of rank and wealth began to use them and place them in their coffins in the Eleventh and Twelfth Dynasties [ca. 2040-1785 B.C.E.]. These are generally known as the Coffin Texts and are called by us The Book of Vindication in accordance with a title given to at least one section of them and in light of a major focus in them. These texts form direct antecedents of many passages and rich imagery in the Book of Coming Forth by Day. The focus on vindication [maa kheru] and transformation [iret kheperu em] dominate and the designation of the departed as Osiris, as in the Pyramid Texts, insures his/her promise of rising, transformation and immortality.

The Book of Coming Forth by Day represents the popularization and mass access to and use of the sacred texts of prayers and aspirations of immortality. The surviving manuscripts are divided into two basic types and periods - the Theban Recension [1575-800 B.C.E.] and the Saite Recension [ca. 664-522 B.C.E.]. The first period represents a process of beginning systemization and yields the best versions of the text. These versions are written on papyri in vertical lines of cursive hieroglyphs and are accompanied by vignettes, beautiful scenes, drawn or painted in various colors to illustrate the text. These vignettes become works of art themselves as shown by the cover of this volume showing the scribe Ani and his wife Tutu. In fact, the papyrus of Ani is, according to Budge [5], "the largest, most perfect and best illuminated of all the papyri containing copies of the Theban Recension...". Finally, the inscriptions of these papyri were further enhanced by the use of red ink to highlight chapter headings or significant points in addition to the use of regular black ink.

The Saite Recension [or Revision] begins in the context of the restoration of order and central authority by kings from the Delta city of Sais in the Twenty-Sixth Dynasty [664-525 B.C.E.]. It is during this revision or recension that a more or less canonical order and content are established. Also, there is a return to a more simple vignette and thus more attention to the text than the art work which at points seemed more important during the Nineteenth Dynasty. In any case, the Book of Coming Forth by Day was clearly the most important sacred text in funerary literature from its first formulation through the Saite period to the end of the Greek period [332-30 B.C.E.].

II. Chapter 125: Philosophical Framework

Of all the engaging sections and chapters in the Book of Coming Forth by Day none is more significant and reflective of Kemetic spirituality than Chapter 125. Here one finds theology and ethics, a philosophical anthropology and eschatology, hymns of praise and declarations of innocence from offenses to God, humans and nature. It is here that one gets not only a concept of ancient Egyptian religion in general, but also and especially important for this work, a concept of the ancient Egyptian ethical ideal as expressed in the Declarations of Innocence.

The essential purpose of this volume, then, is to explicate the ethical ideal found in the Declarations of Innocence in terms relevant to modern ethical discourse. But to do this, it is important to begin by delineating the basic philosophical framework out of which the Kemetic ethical ideal evolves, especially the theology and anthropology in which it is based. Also, it is important at the outset to state the basic assumptions with which I approach my subject and upon which I base and develop my presentation.

To begin with, I assume that much of Kemetic sacred writings is symbolic and hides a deeper meaning than the assertions or narratives might first suggest. Secondly, I assume that beneath the mythological narrative lies a rational core of philosophical value. Thirdly, I assume an underlying unity in diversity in spite of the various theological and anthropological concepts which populate the Kemetic conceptual universe. Fourthly, I assume that Coming Forth is more of a theology of aspiration than a book of magic as most egyptologists claim and thus I treat it as such. Fifthly, I assume that the Declarations of Innocence are an ethical ideal and standard of what one should be able to say one has morally achieved on the Day of Judgment rather than a magic formula one says as substitute for moral achievement which most egyptologists assume. Finally, I recognize the alternative positions which challenge my assumptions, but nevertheless assume sufficient grounds for my own.

A. The Principle of Maat

Any discussion of Kemetic spirituality - whether it is theology, anthropology or ethics - must of necessity include, perhaps even begin with, a discussion of Maat. For Maat is the fundamental principle of ancient Egyptian life. It is the fundamental principle of the divine, natural and social order, established by Ra, God, at the time of creation. As Henri Frankfort observed, Maat is "a divine order established at the time of creation and it is manifest in nature as the normalcy of phenomena. . .in society as justice and . . .in an individual's life as truth" [6]. Siegfried Morenz agrees with this, stating that "Maat is right order in nature and society, as established by the act of creation, and hence means according to context what is right, what is correct, law, order, justice and truth" [7].

Maat as rightness in the divine, natural and social sense becomes the unifying principles of existence. And as it states in the sacred texts, it is that which God loves and requires and humans love and request. In fact, it is the essence of God himself. As Queen Hatshepsut notes, Ra loves Maat and "lives by it" [8]. And as will be argued below, Maat is the grounds for the ontological unity between God and humans. Given Maat's importance to the divine, natural and social order, it is imperative that it be "preserved or established in great matters as in small". Thus, as Morenz states, "Maat is not only right order but also the object of human activity" [9].

Maat, then, expresses its importance in its being a standard of rightness and a goal of practice. Therefore, Maat is the standard by which a person is judged in society and the otherworld and it is a self-declared goal or achievement in historical and ethical literature. The literature as will be shown below is full of declarations of virtues, i.e., having done Maat, that which divinities and humans love, and immortality require [10]. Conscious that each will be judged by both history and heaven, humans and God, Maat becomes the measurement of thought, emotion, speech and conduct, and a goal of practice. But in addition, Maat becomes a reward in itself for it builds character and community and insures immortality. Thus, Beka says he has "done good on earth", avoided injuring others, being evil or approving of any evil, and "delighted in speaking truth". For, he continues, "I know well the reward that comes from this on earth from the time of one's first act til the time one reaches the grave." He goes on to say that truth will be his "sure defense. . .on the day when I reach the divine judges" [11].

Maat's opposite is isfet, i.e., untruth, falsehood, disorder. As the Sebait, the Books of Wise Instruction, teach, isfet is the "abomination of God". It may gain ground for a while, but in the end it leads to destruction. As Ptah-Hotep says, "Maat is great and its value is lasting. Although wickedness may gain wealth, wrongdoing has never brought its wares to [a safe] port. In the end it is Maat that endures and enables one to say, it is the legacy of my father [and mother]" [12]. Maat, then, is the lasting legacy. Thus, one should "Speak Maat and do Maat". For it causes one to have an enriched life and is the basic standard by which one is judged by history and heaven.

B. The Philosophical Anthropology

Maatian theology and ethical philosophy carries within it a definite philosophical anthropology, i.e., a definite conception of the human personality. Evolving first as a philosophical portrait of the king, it later developed into a basic way of viewing humans in general. The first outlines of it are in the so-called Pyramid Texts or the Book of Rising and

Transformation and evolved in a context of great human achievement. As James Breasted notes, such impressive achievement in the basic disciplines of human knowledge and in social construction greatly expanded human vision and the concept of human possibility in ancient Egypt [13].

The rulers and nobles of Egypt clearly saw in their achievement, evidence of both divine favor and a similarity to the divine in their ability to create. They thus had an expanded vision of the human person which to many egyptologists seemed both arrogant and starkly different from the view of humans in their Judeo-Christian anthropology - even though there are at points similarities. Maatian philosophical anthropoplogy or the Kemetic conception of the human personality is grounded in several fundamental propositions. These include: 1] the divine image of humans; 2] the perfectability of humans; 3] the teachability of humans; 4] the free will of humans; and 5] the essentiality of moral social practice in human development.

1. The Divine Image of Humans

The Maatian conception of the human person begins with the proposition that humans are in the image of God. As Kheti says, "they are in his image and came from his body" [14]. This basic understanding carries within it several attendant conceptions. First, inherent in this conception is the assumption that human nature is endowed by Ra and is essentially good, for it is in his likeness. Secondly, then, there is no need for religious transformation, i.e., conversion or salvation. For the divine nature is already there, it simply has to be cultivated through teaching and Maatian social practice. Moreover, then, there is no conception of original sin, i.e., an existential defect as in Judeo-Christian anthropology. That is to say, one is not born in sin, but in the context of possibility. Therefore, offenses to God, humans and nature can be corrected by teaching and self-corrective practice and do not require confession and conversion, or divine grace to an unworthy and inherently sinful being.

Also, the concept of being in the image of God points to the spiritual aspect of the human personality as distinct from the physical. It is the spiritual that is the higher self and belongs to heaven, i.e., the higher plane, whereas the physical belongs to earth. As the texts say: "the soul [belongs] to heaven, the body to earth"; "your essence is in heaven; your body is for earth" (15). Or again the texts say, "I am Lord of the heights and I have made my nest in the sky. But I come down to earth that I may do away with my uncleanliness" (16). Thus, Louis Zabkar's claim of a Kemetic monistic concept of a simple physical body (17) is incorrect and contradicted by the evidence.

2. The Perfectability of Humans

Secondly, the Maatian conception of the human person posits the perfectability of humans. This is not in the sense of finished moral product, but in the sense of progressive development; perpetual becoming and the possibility of assimilation with God as expressed in the Book of Coming Forth by Day and other books of rising like Ra. Thus, Ptah-

Hotep teaches, "Strive for excellence in all you do so that no fault can be found in your character" [18]. Furthermore, he directs his teachings to those who "wish [their] conduct to be perfect", thereby expressing an assumption of human perfectability. The concept of khepert or "becoming" in Kemetic anthropology is essential, for it reveals a conception of and commitment to the progressive perfection of humans. It is this assumption of the possibility of human perfectability that egyptologists decry and question in both the Declarations of Virtue and the Declarations of Innocence. For they fail to see it is more aspiration than announcement and evolves from a concept of progressive perfection rather than one of static perfection. In a word, it is an unfolding and becoming at ever higher levels, not a finished state of static completion.

Also, the concept of perfectability contains within it the concept of the assimilation with God. Throughout the books of rising like Ra, i.e., Coming Forth, Vindication, etc., one finds prayers or declarations of becoming one with God after being judged righteous. For Maat, as argued below, is the grounds of common substance and unity. And to be truly righteous is to be one with God, to share in his spiritual essence. Thus, assimilation with God is also posited conceptually in the Sebait, namely in the Book of Amenomope. Here Amenomope equates the just defender of the wretched with God-likeness, saying, "Surely, the strength of one who is like God saves the wretched from the oppressor."

3. The Teachability of Humans

A third conceptual pillar of the Maatian conception of the human person is his/her teachability. The Sebait, the Books of Wise Instruction, are dedicated to the proposition that the human person is malleable, teachable, capable of moral cultivation which leads to his/her higher self. As Lichtheim notes, the Sebait "at all times. . . [were] inspired by the optimistic belief in the teachability of man" (19). Also, Frankfort states that "the great popularity of the 'teachings' [Sebait] is in itself revealing". The Egyptians were evidently convinced that the good life could be taught" (20). It is, he concludes, "a conviction [which] betrays a surprising confidence in the efficacy of man's understanding" and above all his/her transformability. This, as he notes, is in noticeable contrast to the theology and anthropology of Mesopotamia and Israel where anxiety and doubts about the transformability of humans and their fate was the rule.

It is important here to note that teaching and its correlative learning were always directed toward wisdom. And wisdom in Kemet was always moral wisdom in the service of social and human good. Thus, Ankhsheshonqi says, "It is in the development of character that instruction succeeds" (21).

4. Free Will of Humans

A fourth basic concept in the Kemetic view of the human person is her or his free will. This is expressed in the so-called Coffin Texts or Book of Vindication by the Creator who says, "I did not command them [humans] to do evil. It was their hearts and minds which caused them to disobey that which I commanded" [22]. Thus, humans are free to act as they will and they may choose Maat or isfet, good or evil. But the choice is theirs and they must bear the moral responsibility for their choice. A negative act brings a negative consequence, but humans are rewarded for righteousness. This is the law of reciprocity expressed in the Book of Kheti which says, "A blow struck is repayed by a similar one. For to every action there is a response" [23]. And Khun-Anup says, "Doing Maat is breath to the nose" which expresses the reciprocity of right action which is life [24]. Likewise, Kheti says, "Do Maat that you might live long upon the earth" [25].

Key to the responsible exercise of free will is moral conscience which the ancient Egyptian conceived as rooted in the heart called "ib" or "haty". Actually "ib" or "haty" means both heart and mind and is used in the sacred texts as moral conscience [26]. As early as Ptah-Hotep, the heart had become the moral conscience as Breasted notes. Breasted gives several ways the heart is used to express its role in human life. For the herald of Thutmose III, the heart was a guide in his affairs, "an excellent witness", "an oracle of God in everybody" and "a guide to the good way of achievement". Finally, as Breasted observes, it came to mean "the god that is in you" [27]. And it is this same heart which the ancient Egyptians believed would bear witness in vindication of a person on the Day of Judgment or indict her or him.

Thus, one of the prayers in Coming Forth concerning the heart says: "Stand not up against me as a witness nor oppose me in the Council of Judgment. Weigh not heavy against me before the Keeper of the Balance. May it be favorable to us and there be joy at the weighing of words" (28).

5. The Essentiality of Moral Social Practice

A final fundamental concept in Maatian philosophical anthropology is the essentiality of moral social practice in human development. As argued earlier, Maat is that which endures and raises a person and people up, but isfet leads to destruction. Maat, as social practice, serves several functions in human development. First, it is the basic means by which the affinity of God and humans is expressed. Maat is the essential substance and sustenance of God and humans as expressed in earlier Kemetic anthropology which equated God and King. Thus, Queen Hatshepsut, expressing this affinity, says "I have made bright Maat which he [Ra] loves. I know he lives by it. It is my bread and I eat of its brightness [also]. [For] I am a likeness from his limbs; one with him" (29). Maat, then, is both the nourishment and essence of God and to practice it is to share in his essence and be in harmony with his desire for the world. Therefore, Maat is the grounds for ontological unity and affinity of God and humans and again the grounds of human potential for perfectability, i.e., moral and spiritual development which leads to assimilation with God. Given this, one does not find in Kemetic theology the deep and enduring gap between God and humans which one finds in other theological anthropologies, such as Judaism, Christianity and Orthodox Islam.

Erik Hornung is correct in arguing that Maat also "symbolizes the partnership of God and Man which is brought to fruition in Egyptian religion" [30]. But he is mistaken when he identifies the common task of God and humans as one of maintaining their own existence. For the overwhelming witness of the text is that the shared task of God and humans is one of maintaining Maat in the world. This, in turn, means maintaining the creation and the rightness and righteousness of the order this implies and necessitates. Thus, the texts repeat over and over again each king and queen's commitment to restoring, establishing and expanding Maat. Morenz cites the Book of Rising and Transformation (Pyramid Texts) which reaffirms this. It says, "Heaven is at peace and earth is in joy, for they have heard that [the king] will set Maat in the place of isfet, i.e., right in the place of wrong, order in the place of disorder" [31]. Also, Morenz quotes Tutankhamon's restoration stela which states: "Tutankhamon drove out disorder from the Two Lands and Maat is firmly established in its place; he made lying [grg] an abomination and the land is as it was at the first time," i.e., the time of creation. Creation, then, is constantly threatened by chaos, disorder, or isfet, and humans are morally compelled to share the responsibility with God of defending the boundaries of good, right and order, and expanding them. In this activity humans become like God.

Finally, the Maatian stress on moral social practice is rooted in the assumption that self-actualization of humans is best achieved in morally grounded relations with others. As with other African anthropologies, Maatian anthropology asserts that the perfectability and authenticity of the human person lies in her/his sociality, i.e., rootedness in social relations and practice. Maatian ethics, like African ethics in general, then, stress the practical dimension. Maat or righteousness, is only real in personal/social practice [32]. One must do Maat, i.e., speak truth, do justice and walk each day in the way of righteousness. Maat, then, is a personal and social task, a "lived concreteness" which develops the Maatian person in the context and process of building and sustaining a Maatian society.

The operative principle here is self-realization and grounding in moral relations with others. It is at this point that the ethic of care and responsibility or rather of love in the most human sense [merut] and service [wenut] are evident and required in Maat. To serve is to benefit not only others but also oneself. As the Book of Ankhsheshonqi [33] teaches, service is righteous action towards and for God, humans and by extension, nature which in some meaningful and moral way returns a reciprocal benefit. But Ankhsheshonqi cautions that the only real good deed is the one done for one who needs it. Therefore, he admonishes, that one should not be disappointed for not being recognized or thanked by everyone for whom one does good. For he says, "If you do good by a hundred persons and just one of them acknowledges it, no part of it is lost". Moreover, he states in full moral optimism concerning the certainty of the law of reciprocity, that one should "do a good deed and throw it in the water and when the water dries up, you will find it." One finds a parallel advice in the Hebrew Book of Ecclesiastes which says "Cast your bread upon the waters and after many days it will return to you" (34). Finally, Ankhsheshonqi poses giving, in this case serving, as morally enriching and superior to being given (or served). For he says, "Sweeter is the water of one who has given than the wine of one who has received."

C. The Concept of Immortality

Central to the theology in the Book of Coming Forth By Day is the concept and aspiration of eternal life through righteousness. In fact, the title of the Book itself is a reflection and affirmation of this central and ancient spiritual quest. As early as the Pyramid Texts, there is written evidence of the ancient Egyptian rejection of death as the end of life. On the contrary, death itself was called "repeating life" (wehem ankh). Thus, as Budge states, "the attainment of a renewal of life in the other world was the aim and object of every Egyptian believer" (35). As evidence he cites from the Pyramid Texts passages which declare that King Unas has not gone as one dead, but as one living to sit on the throne of Osiris (The Risen Savior). Having absorbed divine knowledge and been justified by history and heaven, "his existence is forever; his limit is eternity."

Also in Coming Forth, we read: "O Lord Osiris (The Risen Savior and Son of Ra), come then and establish me and make me strong. Grant that I may enter the land of everlastingness as you have done with your father Ra, whose body never passed away and who is one who indeed does not die. I have not done that which you hate, but have praised your name among those who love your Divine Essence. May your spirit love me and not reject me. And may you not let my body decay, but deliver me as you did deliver yourself. Let life rise out of death. Let not decay make an end of me or my enemies come against me in their many forms" (36).

Much has been written about Kemetic belief in the resurrection of the physical body as evidenced by the practice of mummification and even the passage cited above. But although there are passages about the body not decaying and about one knitting oneself back together bone by bone and member by member, there are also passages which stress that it is the spirit that is immortal and that "the body belongs to earth and the soul to heaven" (37). Thus, Budge is correct in asserting that "the preservation of the corruptible body. . .was in some way connected with life in the world to come, and its existence was necessary to insure eternal life, otherwise the prayers recited to this end would have been futile and the time-honored custom of mummifying the dead would have no meaning." But it is still not clear why the preservation of the body was necessary. A plausible explanation is that the ancient Egyptians believed that the various physical and spiritual parts of the human personality - ka, ba, khat, sekem, akh, ren, ib, and shuit" were bound together inseparably and the welfare of any single one of them concerned the welfare of all" (38). Thus, what one has here is a complex set of beliefs which unite the physical and spiritual in a holistic conception of reciprocal effect. It is a topic which obviously requires much more research and analysis and which unfortunately space and announced focus will not allow here.

However, in spite of the complex and often esoteric character of the theology of eternal life, which is expressed in the concept of "coming forth", it can be discussed under five basic analytical categories: a) resurrection; b) ascension; c) judgment; d) acceptance; and e) transformation. To come forth by day, from the darkness of death and the tomb to the light and eternal life of the other world is the hinge and hub on which the teachings on immortality turn. As I stated above, coming forth is essentially breaking the bonds of death and grave and emerging to bask in sunlight, i.e., the rays of Ra in the spiritual sense. This is resurrection, rising from the dead and repeating life through righteousness. In the Book of Vindication, we read "O' seeker of vindication, the earth opens its mouth for you; it opens its jaws in your behalf. May you reach the Great Stairway and arrive at the Sacred City" (39). Also, it says "The Lord of the earth will open your blind eyes and straighten out your bent knees for you. And you will be given your heart which came from your mother [and] belongs to your body, and your soul which was on earth...." Thus, the departed are resurrected and they pray as in the Book of Coming Forth By Day, "May I not be judged according to the mouth of the multitude. May my soul lift itself up before my heart and be found to have been righteous on earth. May I come into your presence O' Lord of Lords; may I reach the Hall of Righteousness [Maati]. May I rise like a living god and give forth light like the divine powers that are in heaven."

Secondly, then, the concept of immortality or coming forth involves ascension, i.e., rising like Ra, ascending into heaven to be judged and transformed into an imperishable spirit, i.e., a netcher. Again, in the Book of Vindication, one reads: "Hail vindicated one. Come that you may rise up in the heavens. The ladder at the side of Ra has been assembled for you among the powers of heaven.... You shall walk upon your own feet and you shall not walk with your head downward." Or again we read: "The doors of heaven are opened [to you] because of your righteousness. May you ascend and see Hathor. May any case against you be cancelled" (40). Also, in the Book of Rising and Transformation or Pyramid Texts, it says, "Rise up O' vindicated one. Take hold of your head. Gather together your bones, collect your limbs and shake the dust from your flesh.... Stand at the gates that bar those with no name. Lo, the gatekeeper comes out to you. He takes hold of your hand and takes you to heaven to your Father." Finally, we read that through righteousness the departed "fl[ies] up to heaven in the company of my brothers and sisters, the powers of heaven,"(41) using his/her arms like wings of a hawk. Thus, three images of ascension emerge here: one of a ladder or stairway being placed for the departed to ascend; the departed's rising as a spirit, and finally, his/her rising by flying to heaven like a hawk, an obvious reference to Horus, son of Osiris the Risen Savior, and whose symbol is the hawk. But regardless of the symbolic analogy used, ascension remains at the heart and center of coming forth.

Thirdly, coming forth involves judgment in the Great Hall of Maati. Here king, queen, noble and the common person had to justify themselves and be vindicated (maa kheru, true of voice and triumphant) in their quest for immortality by a valid claim of a righteous life on earth. As the Declarations of Innocence and Virtues reveal, one had to be free of offenses against God, humans and nature (animate and inanimate) and to have done positive acts of good especially to the vulnerable. Upon arriving at the Great Hall of Maati, one enters humbly, bowing as scenes from the Papyrus of Ani, the scribe, and Tutu, his wife, show. In one scene Ani appeals to his heart not to betray him, i.e., not to have misled him in his assumption of righteousness. As other papyri demonstrate and as noted above, the risen one, then, declares her/himself innocent of all offenses and asserts her/his having done good in the sight of God and humans, before history and heaven. This two-pronged justification is important for it shows the Maatian concern with not simply not doing evil, but also in doing good. Or put another way, as Khun-Anup says of the righteous person, s/he is not only "one who destroys isfet [evil]", but also "one who brings righteousness [Maat] into being" (42).

After one declares both innocence and virtue, one's heart is placed in the Great Scale of Judgment, where one's heart is weighed against the feather of Maat. Anpu (Anubis), the netcher (43) of the departed, is Master of the Scales (iry mekhat) and conducts the weighing. Jehuti (Thoth), Lord of Just Measure and Scribe of Heaven, records and announces the verdict to the Forty-Two Assessors. He says,

"Hear this word in truth. I have judged the heart of Osiris [Ani]. His soul stands as a witness [for] him. His character is just according to the Great Scales. And no fault has been found in him." They, in turn, affirm his ruling saying, "What you have said is true. The Osiris Ani, justified, is righteous. He has committed no offense nor has he done anything against us. Ammit shall not be permitted to have power over him." If, however, the one judged is not judged "maa kheru" - vindicated, true of voice and triumphant - s/he is turned over to Ammit (Ammut, the Devourer of the Dead) who dispatches him/her into non-existence.

Having been judged maa-kheru, one becomes an Osiris - as the quote above shows and like Osiris himself, gains eternal life. Eternal life is thus, closely connected to Osiris, the Risen Savior and Son of Ra, who was killed and resurrected and through his resurrection in and through righteousness represents the possibility and promise of eternal life through righteousness (Maat). Therefore, having been ruled righteous by Jehuti and the Forty-Two Netchers, Ani is lead by Horus, son of Isis and Osiris, before Osiris. Here Horus reports that Ani has been found righteous in the Scales and requests he be accepted among the powers of heaven. Ani then says to Osiris, "Behold I am in your presence O' Lord of Heaven. There is no evil in my body. I have not knowingly spoken that which is not true, nor have I done anything with a false heart. Grant that I may be like those favored ones who are in your following and that I may be an Osiris and greatly favored by the Beneficent God." Then he kneels before Osiris, presents his offerings and is received into paradise or heaven.

Fourthly, acceptance and welcome into the company of God and his following, then, is a part of the larger process of coming forth. An important prayer in the Book of Coming Forth says: "May the Lords of the Sacred Land receive me and give me threefold praise in peace. May they make a seat for me besides the Elder of the Council. May I ascend in the presence of the Beneficent One [Osiris]. And may I assume whatever form I want in whatever place my spirit wishes to be" (44). Also, one reads, as cited above, "Grant that I may be like those favored ones who are in your following and that I may be an Osiris [one vindicated and risen] and greatly favored by the Beneficent God." Moreover, we read in the sacred writings where the vindicated one is commanded to go take his/her place among the netchers. "Go and open the mansion of the soul beyond. . . . If you find the powers of heaven seated, you shall sit with them. Receive then this scepter of yours which is at the feet of Ra and your rod which is at the feet of the morning star." And another prayer in <u>Coming Forth</u> says: as "I am one whose mouth is pure and whose hands are clean. . .let it be said to me: 'Welcome come in peace' by those who shall see me."

Finally, the vindicated one is transformed into a living spirit in the process of coming forth. S/he is Osiris, one with Ra, and any other netcher s/he wishes to be. As quoted above, the prayer is "May I assume whatever form I want, in whatever place my spirit wishes to be" (45). Or again, the sacred writings say, having been vindicated, "I stand up like Horus, [beloved son and avenger of his father]. I sit down as Ptah [Creator who laid the foundations of the universe]. I have grown as strong as Jehuti [wisdom exalted]. I have become as powerful as Atum [Ra as the perfecter]. I have entered as a falcon and come forth as a phoenix. Morning star make way for me, so that I may adore Ra in the [beautiful paradise of] the West." Also, we read the vindicated declaring now, "I am s/he who is one with God. I have become He." Or "I shine like Ra daily. I establish truth and expel falsehood. I open the doors which are in the abyss below."

And finally, we read in the sacred writings the vindicated saying s/he has been transformed into a series of mighty spirits. This is, as all of the above, assimilation with God and the divine through righteousness and an aspiration to transform oneself into any form in any place one's spirit wishes to be. Thus, we read the vindicated one declaring, "I am the Lion, the Double Lion and the greatest of his [her] priesthood. I am Horus, the Uniter. I am he [she] who brings stillness after the storm. I am Isis in Chemmis [taking refuge from Seth, the evil one] and I will listen like one who is deaf and strains to see. I am Lord of the Earth, who entered the earth. I am he [she] who evaluates whoever serves him [her]. I am transformed into one whose spirits are mighty (italics mine]. I am one with Ra, Lord of His Two Lands, and am he [she] who is put behind Him. I am the waters and the earth."

It is in this philosophical framework outlined above, then, that the spiritual and ethical meaning of the Book of Coming Forth By Day becomes evident. For coming forth is essentially a spiritual aspiration for eternal life and the spiritual power and freedom to be and do whatever one wishes in whatever place one's spirit desires to be. Or as Naville [46] states, coming forth "is to be delivered from that decreed and determined duration of time pertaining to every earthly life, and to have existence with neither beginning nor end, without limits in time and space." In a word, "it is to be delivered from these limits", rise like Ra and declare with power and permanent certainty born of righteousness that: "Ra has received me unto himself, to heaven, to the eastern side of the heavens, as Horus the Avenger of his father, as Osiris the Risen One, as this star which lights up the sky. My sister is Sirius and my offspring is the morning star. Never again will the heavens be void of me or the earth be empty of my presence" [47].

Notes

1. The "e" inserted between the consonants are simply conventional insertions to facilitate pronunciation.

2. Thomas Allen. The Book of the Dead or Going Forth By Day, Chicago: University of Chicago Press, 1974.

3. Maulana Karenga. Selections From The Husia: Sacred Wisdom of Ancient Egypt, Los Angeles: University of Sankore Press, 1984, p. 106.

4. Ibid., p. 118ff.

5. E.A. Wallis Budge. The Book of the Dead, New York: University Books, 1960, p. 106.

6. Henri Frankfort. Ancient Egyptian Religion, New York: Harper and Row, 1948, p. 6

7. Siegfried Morenz. Egyptian Religion, Ithaca, New York: Cornell University, 1978, p. 113.

8. Henri Frankfort. Kingship and the Gods, Chicago: University of Chicago Press, 1969, p. 158.

9. Morenz, op. cit., p. 113.

10. Karenga, The Husia, pp. 93ff.

11. Ibid., p. 97.

12. Ibid., p. 64.

13. James Breasted. The Dawn of Conscience, New York: Charles Scribner's & Sons, 1934, p. 44.

14. Husia, p. 41.

15. Budge, op. cit., p. 68.

16. Husia, p. 108.

17. Louis Zabkar, "Some Observations on T.G. Allen's Edition of The Book of the Dead," Journal of Near Eastern Studies, 24, 1 & 2, (January-April, 1965) pp. 75-87.

18. Husia, p. 101ff.

19. Miriam Lichtheim, Ancient Egyptian Literature, Volume I, Berkeley: University of California Press, 1973, p. 6.

20. Frankfort, (1948) op cit., p. 60.

21. Husia, p. 64, 48.

22. Husia, pp. 8-9.

23. Lichtheim, op. cit., p. 105.

24. Husia, p. 32.

25. Husia, p. 51.

26. Alexandre Piankoff. Le Coeur dans les Textes Egyptiens, Paris: Librarie Orientaliste, aul Geuthner, 1930.

27. Breasted, op. cit., p. 254.

28. Husia, p. 106.

29. Frankfort, (1948) p. 158.

30. Erik Hornung. Conceptions of God in Ancient Egypt, Ithaca, New York: Cornell University Press, 1971, pp. 215-216.

31. Morenz, op. cit., p. 114.

32. Morenz, op. cit., 114.

33. Maulana Karenga. "Towards A Sociology of Maatian Ethics: Literature and Context" in Maulana Karenga (ed.) Reconstructing Kemetic Culture, Los Angeles: University of Sankore Press, 1990, pp. 66-96.

34. "The Book of Ecclesiastes," The Bible.

35. Budge, op. cit., p. 66ff.

36. Husia, p. 108.

37. Budge, op. cit., p. 81.

38. Ibid., p. 81.

39. Husia, p. 113, 114, 105-106.

40. Husia, p. 115.

41. Husia, p. 118ff.

42. Husia, p. 31.

43. Netcher may be translated as God, god, Lord, lord or as a power or principle in nature or heaven.

43. Husia, p. 106, 107, 115, 112.

45. Husia, p. 45, 107-108, 116, 117.

46. Edourd Naville. The Old Egyptian Faith, New York: G.P. Putnam's Sons, 1906, p. 165.

47. Husia, p. 122.

SECTION II - TEXT AND TRANSLATION

Declarations of Innocence

The hieroglyphic transcription which follows is that of E.A. Wallis Budge in The Book of the Dead, New York: University Books, 1960. Although many of his transcriptions are faulty due to the level of the field at that time, he is often correct and still provides more of the original hieroglyphs than any other of the egyptologists. This alone is worthy of credit, especially given the tendency of egyptologists to render the field an almost closed and exclusive area of study.

My translation of the text has made valuable use of the existing translations and studies of the Book of Coming Forth, especially those in English and French and the more recent ones. Some of these are: Thomas G. Allen, The Book of the Dead, 1974; R.O. Faulkner, The Book of the Dead, 1985; Miriam Lichtheim, "Chapter 125", Ancient Egyptian Literature, Volume II, 1976; Evelyn Rossiter, The Book of the Dead, 1979; J.A. Wilson, Chapter 125 in Ancient Near Eastern Texts, 1969; Charles Mayster, Les Declarations D'Innocence [Livre Des Morts, Chap. 125], 1937; Paul Barquet, Le Livre des Morts de ancien Egyptiens, 1967; and Etienne Drioton, "Contribution A L'Etude du Chapitre CXXV du Livre des Morts: Les Confessions Negative", among others.

Where Budge's transcriptions were faulty, I simply translated them according to modern restorations or readings. Also, where sentences would be enhanced by additional words for clarification, I added them in brackets. Moreover, I have left out the more symbolic and mystical parts of the Chapter. For my intent here is to extract and explicate the ethics of the Chapter, not its more esoteric and mystical aspects.

Chapter 2

THE DECLARATIONS OF INNOCENCE

- Chapter 125 -

I. Translation of Text

INTRODUCTION

What one should [be able to] say (1) upon arriving at this Great Hall of Maati, The Two Truths (2) so that he/she may be purified from all wrong-doing which he/she has done and face the Divine Ones without fear (3).

Homage to you Great God, Lord of Maati. I have come before you, my Lord. I was brought that I might behold your beauty. I know you. I know your name. I know the name of the forty-two divini-

Chapter 2

THE DECLARATIONS OF INNOCENCE

- Chapter 125 -

I. The Hieroglyphic Text

INTRODUCTION

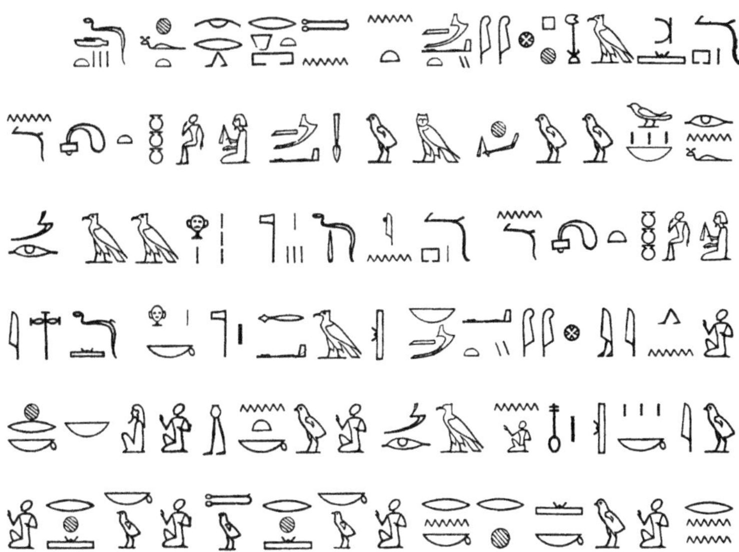

ties who are with you in the Great Hall of Maati, those who live to stand guard against evil doers and who consume their blood (4) on that day of taking account of characters before Wennofer (5). Surely, The Two Daughters, Two Eyes, Lord of Two Truths is your name. Indeed, I have come before you. And I have brought you Maat. I have done away with evil for you.

DECLARATION OF INNOCENCE (A)

1. I have not done wrong to people.

2. I have not impoverished my family or friends. (6)

3. I have not done evil in the place of Righteousness. (7)

4. I have not known that which does not exist. (8)

5. I have not done evil.

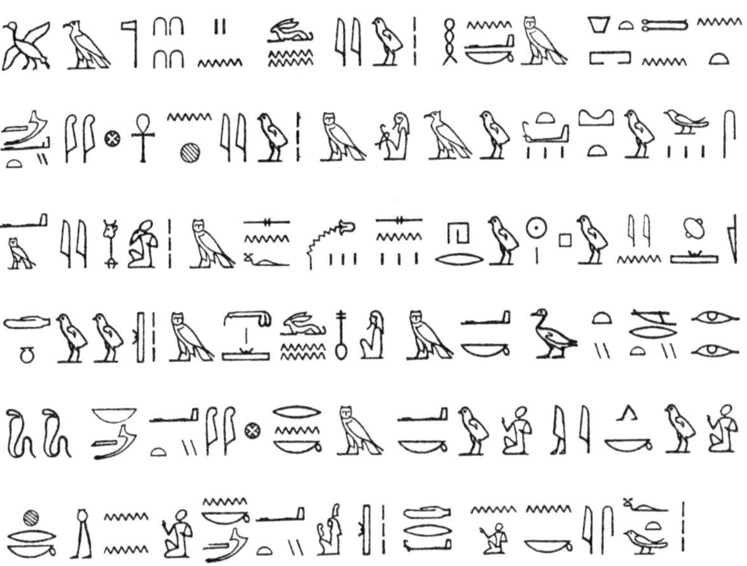

DECLARATION OF INNOCENCE (A)

1.

2.

3.

4.

5.

6. I have not begun the day by demanding more work than is due me.

7. My name has not reached the offices of those who oversee servants.

8. I have not deprived the orphan of his/her property.

9. I have not done what the divine ones hate.

10. I have not slandered a servant to his/her superior.

11. I have not caused anyone pain.

12. I have not caused anyone to hunger.

13. I have not caused anyone to weep.

14. I have not killed anyone.

15. I have not commanded anyone to kill.

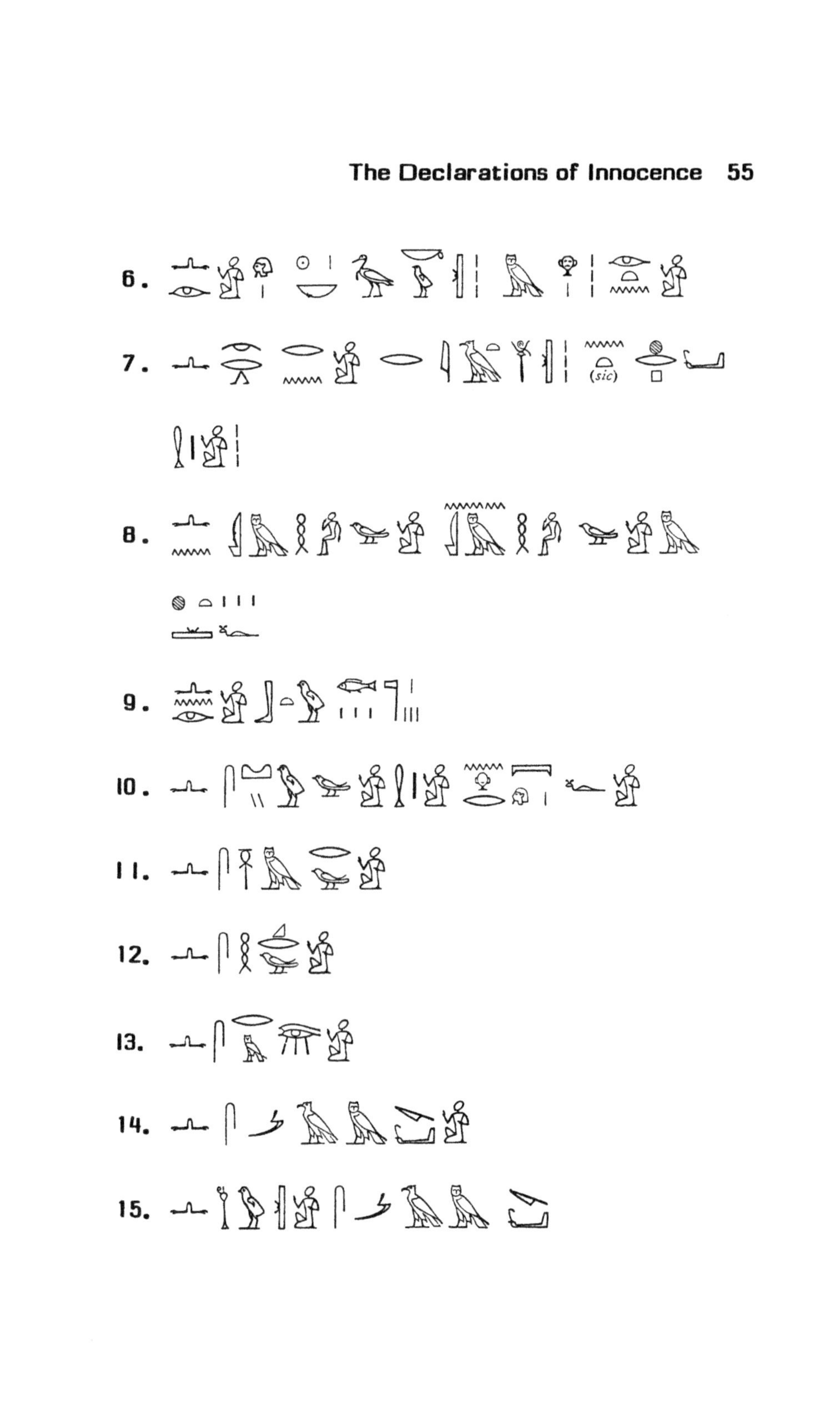

6.

7. (sic)

8.

9.

10.

11.

12.

13.

14.

15.

16. I have not caused anyone to suffer.

17. I have not reduced the food-offerings of the temples.

18. I have not destroyed the loaves of the divine ones.

19. I have not removed the food-offerings of the blessed ones.

20. I have not committed fornication.

21. I have not been unchaste.

22. I have not reduced the funeral offerings.

23. I have not lessened the acre. [10]

24. I have not encroached upon the fields [of others].

25. I have not added to or taken from the weight of the scales.

26. I have not tampered with the tongue of the scales.

16.

17.

18.

19.

20.

21.

22.

23.

24.

25.

26.

27. I have not taken milk from the mouth of children.

28. I have not deprived small cattle of their

pasture.

29. I have not trapped birds in the sacred marshes.

30. I have not caught fish with [the bait of]

their bodies.

31. I have not stopped or diverted the flow of water in its season. (11)

32. I have not damned water when it should flow.

33. I have not put out a fire when it should burn.

34. I have not neglected the days of making meat offerings.

35. I have not driven away cattle upon the property of God.

27.

28.

29.

30.

31.

32.

33.

34.

35.

36. I have not opposed God in his going forth.

I am pure. I am pure. I am pure. I am pure. My purity is the purity of that great phoenix which is in Heracleopolis. For I am indeed the nose of the Lord of Breath who sustains all people on the day of completing the Eye in On [12] on the last day of the second month of winter, in the presence of the lord of this land. Nothing evil will happen to me in this land in this Great Hall of Maati. For I know the names of these divinities which are in it: [the servants of the great God.] [13]

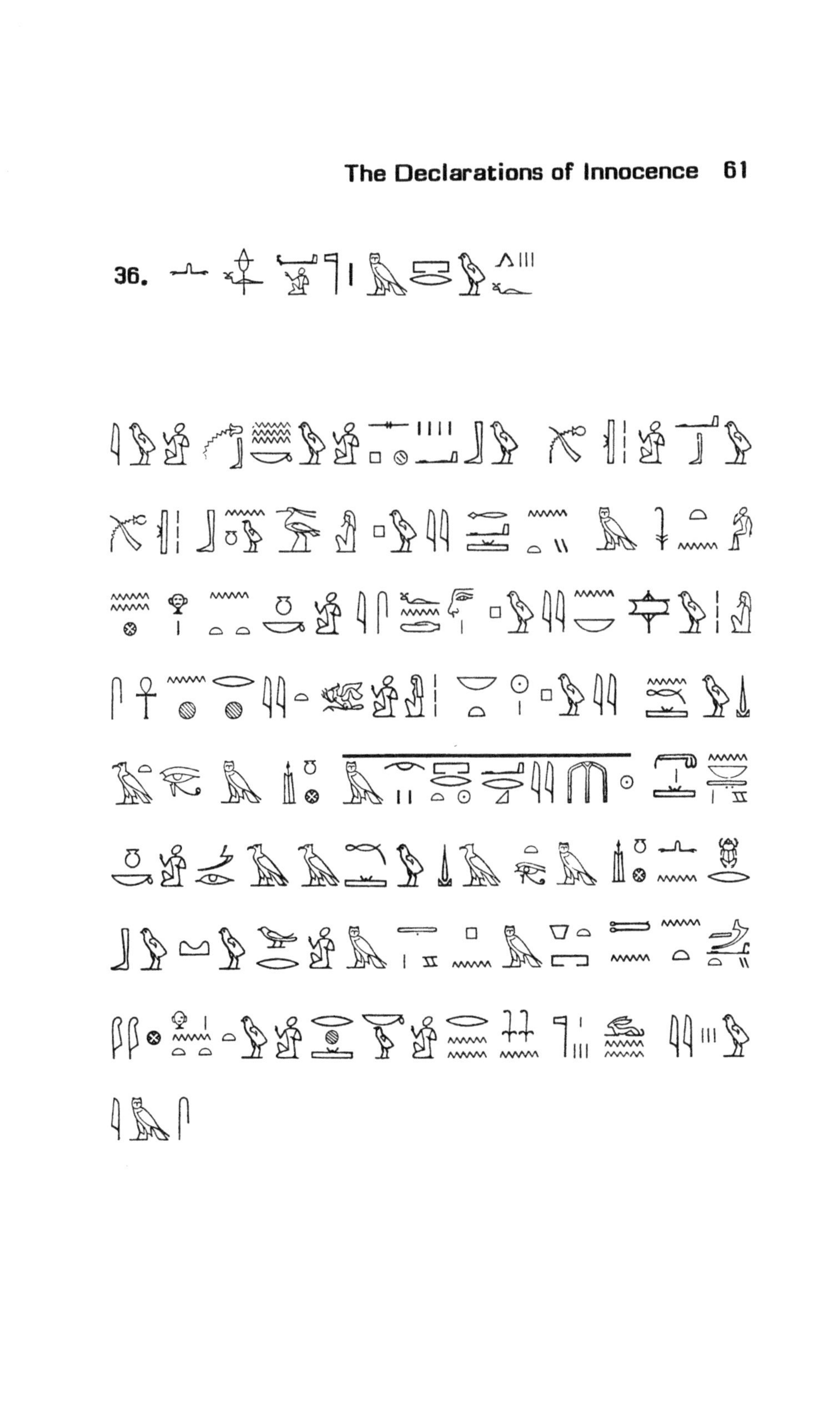

36.

DECLARATION OF INNOCENCE (B)

1. O Wide-Strider who comes forth from Heliopolis, I have not done evil.

2. O Embracer-of-Fire who comes forth from Kheraha, I have not robbed.

3. O Long-Nosed who comes forth from Hermopolis, I have not stolen.

4. O Consumer-of-Shadows who comes forth from the cave, I have not killed people.

5. O Fierce-of-Face who comes forth from Rosetau, I have not destroyed food supplies.

6. O Double-Lion who comes forth from heaven, I have not done fraudulent things.

7. O Flint-Eyed who comes forth from Letopolis, I have not stolen sacred property.

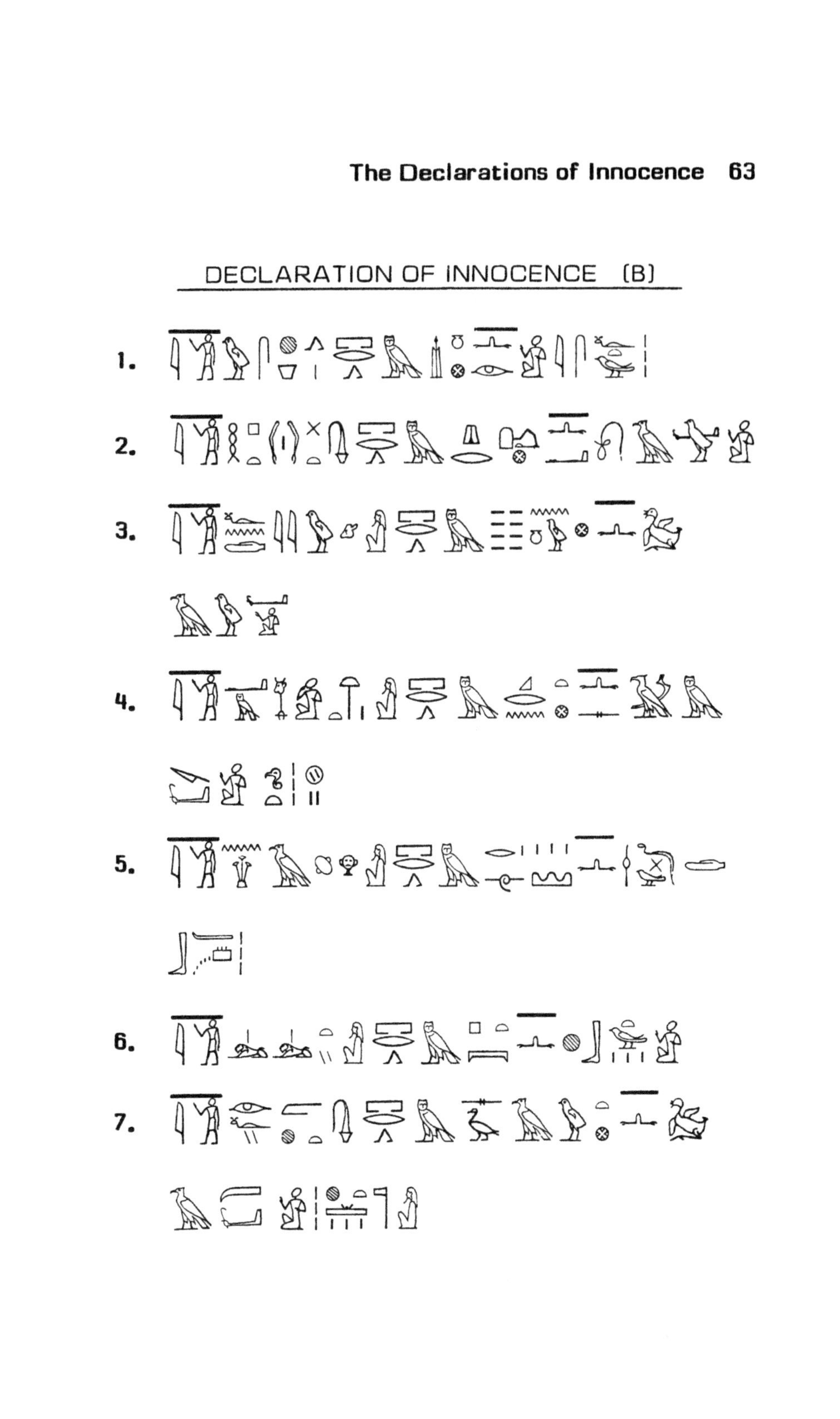

DECLARATION OF INNOCENCE (B)

1.

2.

3.

4.

5.

6.

7.

8. O Fiery-One who comes forth backwards, I have

I have not told lies.

9. O Breaker-of-Bones who comes forth from

Heracleopolis, I have not taken away food.

10. O Flourishing-Of-Flame who comes forth from

Memphis, I have not been sullen.

11. O Cave-Dweller who comes forth from the West, I have not been unchaste.

12. O Backward-Face who comes forth from the Pit, I have not winked [at injustice].

13. O Wanderer who comes forth from Bubastis, I have not been false or dissembled.

14. O' Flame-Footed who comes forth from Dusk, I have not violated [the law].

15. O' Consumer-Of-Blood who comes forth from the place of slaughter, I have not dealt deceitfully.

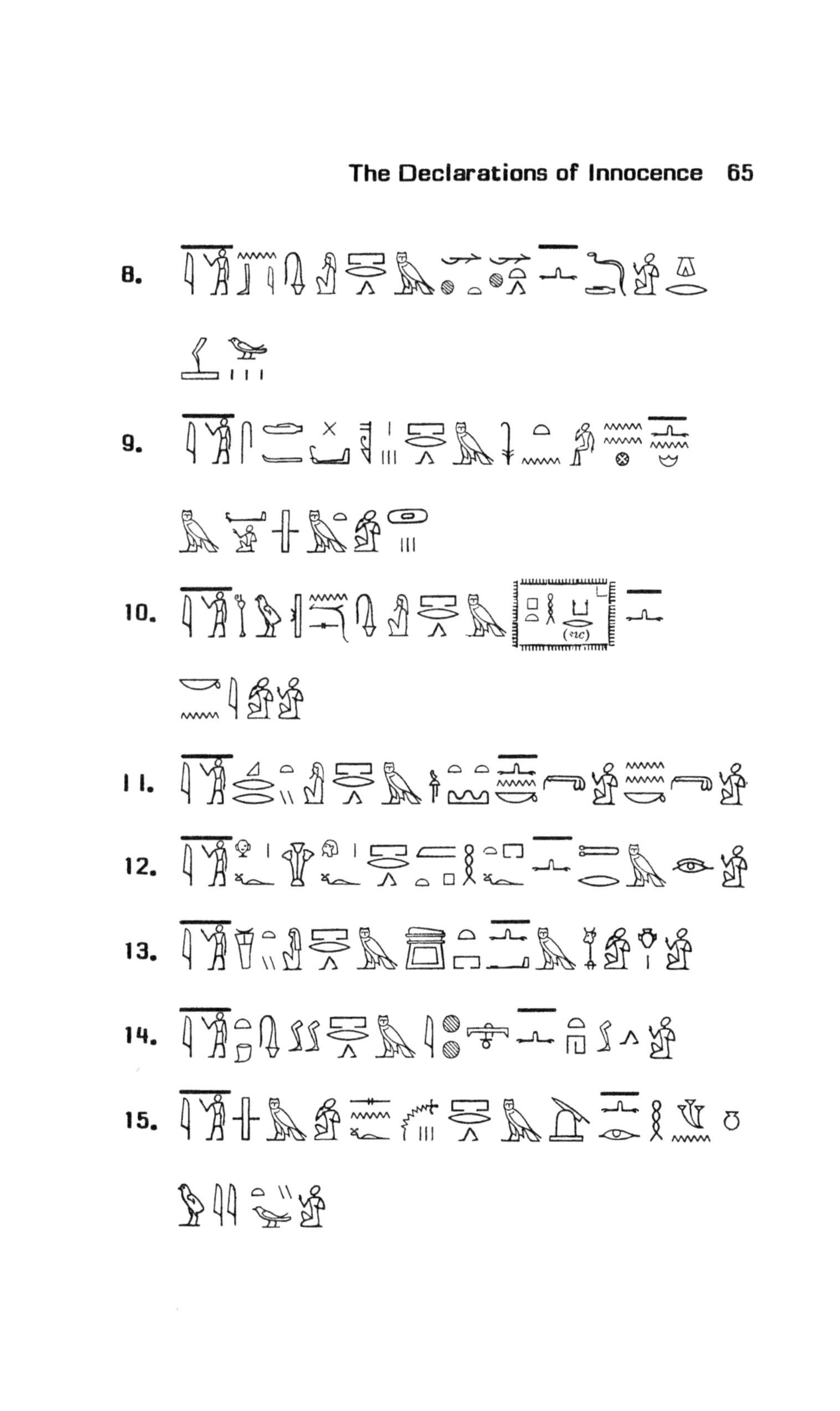

8.

9.

10. (sic)

11.

12.

13.

14.

15.

16. O' Consumer-Of-Entrails who comes forth from the Tribunal of Thirty, I have not stolen cultivated land.

17. O' Lord of Maat who comes from Maaty, I have not eavesdropped.

18. O Wanderer who comes forth from Bubastis, I have not [trespassed].

19. O Pale-One who comes from On, I have not contended except concerning my own goods.

20. O Truly-Evil-One who comes from Andjet, I have not lain with another's wife.

21. O Wememty Snake who comes from the slaughter house, I have not committed adultery

22. O You who see who you bring who comes forth from Min's Temple, I have not been unchaste.

16. 

17.

18.

19.

20.

21.

22.

23. O Chief-Of-The-Elders [Nobles] who comes forth from Djefet, I have not terrorized anyone.

24. O Wrecker who comes forth from Xois, I have not transgressed [the law].

25. O' Disturber who comes forth from Weryt, I have not been hot-tempered.

26. O' Child who comes forth from the nome of On, I have not been deaf to the words of Truth.

27. O Dark One who comes forth from darkness, I have not quarrelled.

28. O Peace-Bringer who comes forth from Sais, I have not been aggressive.

29. O Foreteller of things to come who comes forth from Wensi, I have not caused strife.

30. O One-Of-Many-Faces who comes forth from Ndjefet, I have not been impatient.

31. O Accuser who comes forth from Wetjenet, I have not eavesdropped.

23. 

24.

25.

26.

27.

28.

29.

30.

31.

32. O Horned One who comes forth from Siut, I have not been talkative.

33. O Nefertem who comes forth from Memphis, I have done no evil.

34. O Timeless One who comes forth from Djedu, I have not cursed or opposed the King.

35. O One who acts as he wills who comes forth from Tjebu, I have not waded in water.

36. O One-Who-Treads on water who comes forth from Nun, I have not raised my voice.

37. O Commander of people who comes forth from his Sais, I have not cursed or opposed God.

38. O Provider of Kas who comes forth from his cavern, I have not exalted myself.

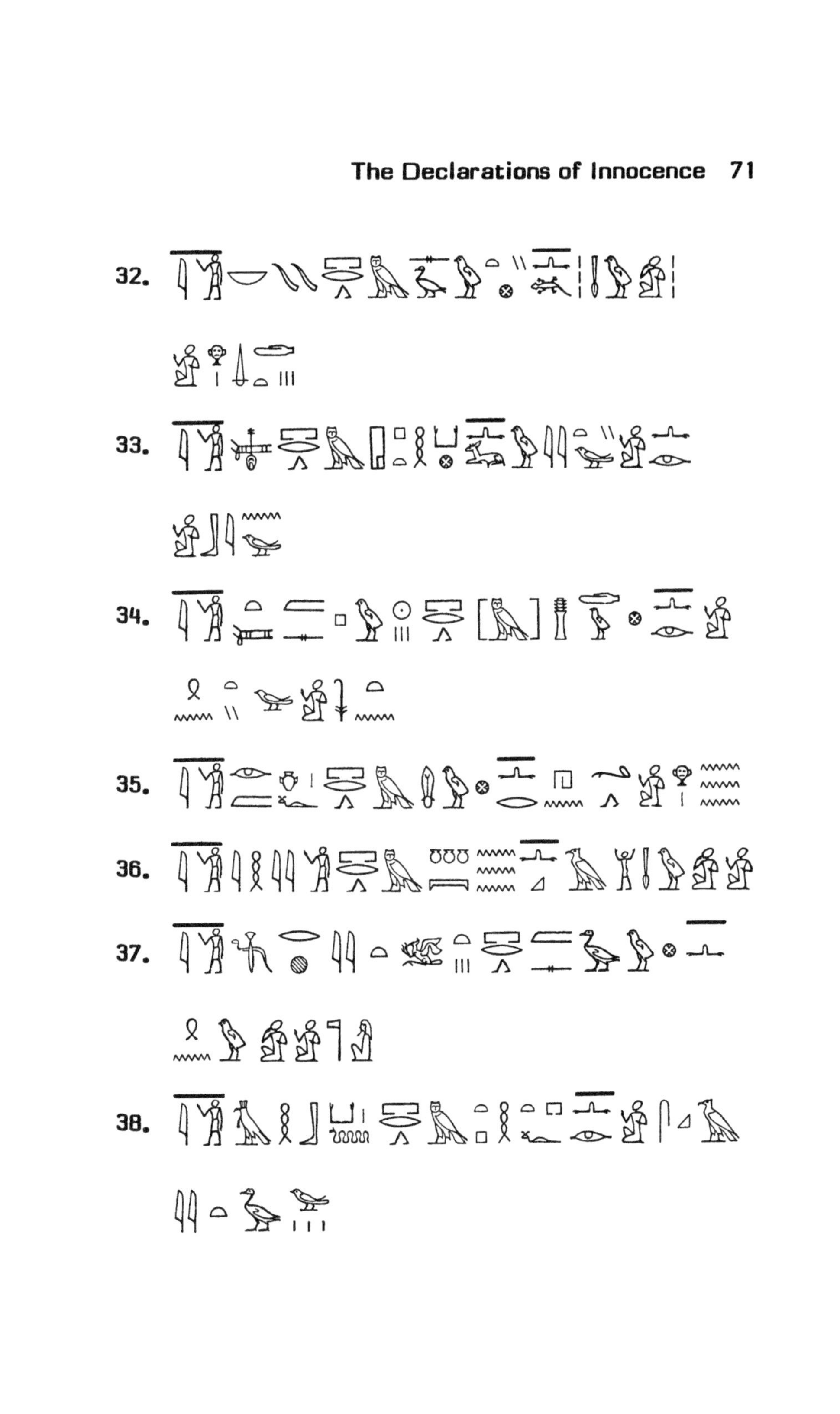

32.

33.

34.

35.

36.

37.

38.

39. O Provider of Good who comes forth from his cavern, I have not stolen [destroyed] divine offerings.

40. O One of Raised Head who comes forth from the cavern, I have not stolen the offerings of the Departed Ones.

41. O One-Who-Brings-and-Gives who comes forth from Maaty, I have not taken bread from a child or blasphemed the God of my city.

42. O White Toothed who comes forth from Lake-land, I have not killed sacred cattle.

ADDRESS TO THE DIVINE ONES

Then shall the heart which is righteous and without fault say: (15)

Homage to you, O you divine ones who are in this Great Hall of Maati. I know you. I know your

39. 

40.

41.

42.

ADDRESS TO THE DIVINE ONES

names. I will not fall in fear of you. You shall not accuse me of wrong to this God whom you serve. No case against me shall come before you. You shall speak truthfully about me before the Lord of All. For I have done what was right in the Beloved Land, Egypt. I have not blasphemed against God. No case against me came before the King during his reign.

Homage to you divine ones of the Great Hall of Maati, who have no lies in their bodies, who live on righteousness, who drink of righteousness before Horus in his disk. Rescue me from Babi who lives

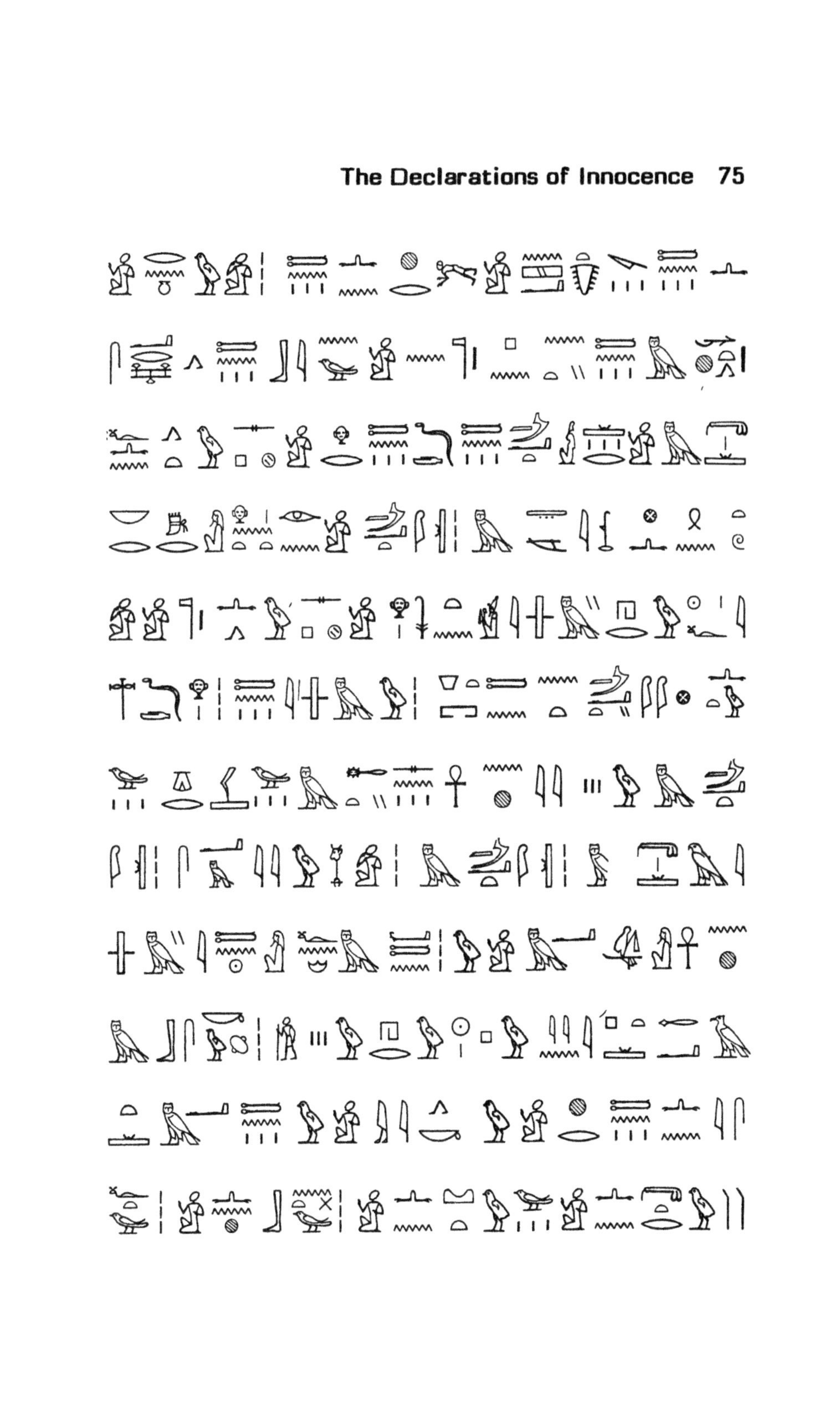

on the entrails of [even] those with high status on this day of Great Reckoning. Behold me, I come before you. Without wrongdoing, without guilt, without evil, without a witness against me, for there is none against whom I have done anything. I live on truth. I drink of truth. I have done what people speak of and that which pleases the divine ones. I have satisfied God with that which he loves. I have given bread to the hungry, water to the thirsty, clothes to the naked and a boat to those without one. I have given divine offerings to the divine ones, and 'nvocation offerings to the departed.

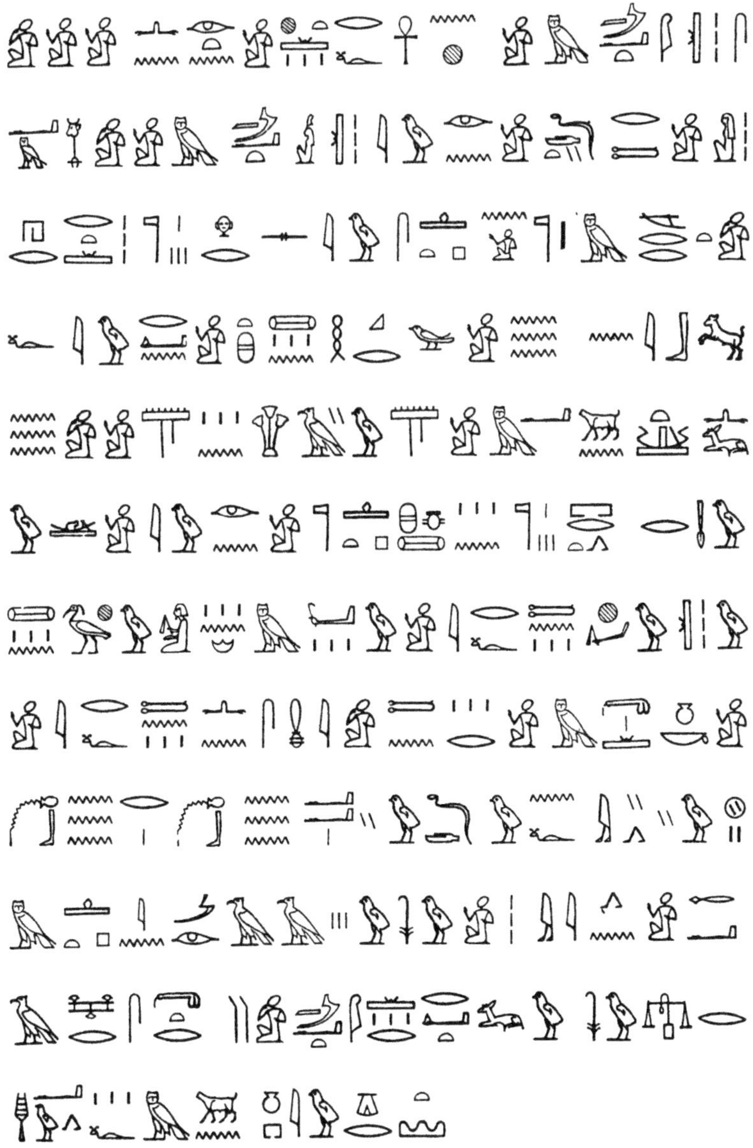

Rescue me, then and protect me. Do not complain against me before the Great God. For I am one whose hands are clean, one to whom it is said, "Welcome, Come in peace" by those who see him/her . . . . Indeed, I have come here to bear witness to the Truth and to set the scales [of justice] in their proper place among those who are silent [or the voiceless]. [16]

Notes

1. I've added "to be able" (to say), because, as I have argued, this is a statement of ethical and spiritual aspiration rather than "magic" as many egyptologists argue.

2. Maati here means both the Two Truths and the "really true" Truth. For "i" on Maat can be the dual or an augmentative, i.e., an indicator of expansion and/or stress. Two Truths may represent the dual character of reality, spiritual, physical and the dualities of life - Good, evil, high, low, strong, weak, etc.

3. I've added "without fear" to further clarify the sense of the statement.

4. "Consume their blood" seems to be a way of saying "drain them of life", in a word, destroy them.

5. Wennofer is Osiris, Lord of the Departed. The name literally means the "Good Being" or "Good One".

6. Wendjut literally means "familiars" and thus "associates, family members, friends, etc."

7. In the place of righteousness can mean instead of righteousness or in court, i.e., seat of justice. The phrase is "m set Maat".

8. That which does not exist is that beyond the realm of the real and ordered. It is chaos be-

yond the boundaries of the ordered world. See more in Section III, commentary.

9. An alternative rendering is "My name has not reached the pilot of the Divine Bark."

10. This is literally an "aroura" (setchat) about two-thirds of an acre. I used acre as a basic and familiar unit in English.

11. "khesef" may mean "divert", "stop" or "block".

12. On is also called Heliopolis.

13. As Budge points out, these words are added in the Papyrus of Ani.

14. The word here seems to be "nwdw" which means act perversely and it is coupled with "nek-nek", copulate. Some translate this as homosexual sex, but perverse sex of any kind appears to be the meaning.

15. This sentence is so phrased to set the context for the declaration which follows.

16. Actually, the sentence literally reads, I've come here to set the scales (of Maat) in their proper place in the land of the silent, which means the land of the departed and refers to the judgment process. However, one can translate it as does Allen, as "set the scales in their proper place among the silent ones." It then symbollically can be used to suggest the living and dead who have no voice. I have chosen the latter symbolic interpretation.

SECTION III - ETHICAL COMMENTARY

Chapter 3

ETHICS: THE SOCIAL, DIVINE AND NATURAL

I. Introduction

The Declarations of Innocence and their accompanying declarations of virtue compose what can be considered an ideal way of life for the ancient Egyptians as well as a standard of moral practice by which they could judge themselves and society. These, in turn, have their roots in two basic sources: the Declarations of Virtue or Ikeru called "ideal biographies" by egyptologists, and the Sebait, the Books of Instruction. These, of course, are all rooted in and reflective of concern for and commitment to the principle and practice of Maat. As noted above in the section on the philsophical framework, Kemetic theology and ethics posit a moral ecology of human possibility. Humans are not ontologically scarred by "sin", but must daily struggle in a cooperative project with the Divine to sustain and expand the boundaries of right and order (Maat) and push back the advance of wrong and chaos (isfet). The key here is moral choice and capacity of the human person to act for the Good, unencumbered by concepts of original or ontological sin, but compelled to remain conscious-in-practice of one's obligation to the human, Divine and natural.

Moreover, one does good not simply because of anticipation of judgment, but also because of the good it brings in turn. In other words, one does good to create and sustain moral community. As Khun-Anup teaches, "Do to the doer that s/he may also do" [Husia:32]. In other words, it means doing good that more good may in turn be done, thus creating a context of ever-expanding good in which all may flourish. Maat or righteousness is seen as the essential constitutive element of being human and thus one strives to practice it in thought, emotion, speech and conduct in order to realize his/her potential fully. And as one can never realize oneself outside the social context, one does right to create and maintain the Maatian society, the just and good society in which the human, Divine and natural merge in a reciprocal relationship of harmony, balance and order. Thus, Ptah-Hotep teaches that Maat is great, lasting and effective and it is not only grounding for oneself but a legacy to leave for future generations. Here the righteous and the beneficial coincide and every act of good returns in kind, creating a moral ecology for ever higher levels of human life.

Given the promising grounds of Kemetic or Maatian ethics, one is led to ask how would or could they serve modern society, especially the world African community as a rescued and revitalized legacy? This work is based on the assumption that the ancient Egyptian ethical texts form a foundation for moral reflection on issues of importance to us as a national and world African community and as fellow humans in a world community of other humans. The task is to recover and reconstruct this ancient Maatian moral legacy and make it real and relevant for modern life. In a world of fast-changing values, it is vitally important that ethical questions of contemporary society be engaged and evaluated from an Afrocentric view, that our evaluations and inquiry be rooted in the cultural image and human interests of African people and that we pose our own paradigm of human possibility.

Maatian ethics pose an excellent challenge to provide an Afrocentric contribution to modern moral discourse. It promises a creative challenge to mainstream religious ethics based on theology and faith or ancient law. For Maatian ethics respects the Divine but does not engage in theological disputes and has no all-embracing laws which leave little or less room for creative thought about new and ongoing challenges to the African and human community. Maatian ethics emphasizes moral behavior and character development over claims of theology, faith, commandments and laws. The hinge on which Maatian and indeed all African ethics turn is the quality of human relations and human practice in the context of the social, the Divine and the natural. Thus, to discuss Maatian ethics critically as outlined in the Declarations of Innocence, we can divide them into three broad categories of moral concern: the social, the Divine and the natural.

II. The Social

The social concerns of Maatian ethics are the quality of human relations and the development of character necessary to initiate and sustain quality relations and a moral community in which they are cultivated and reinforced. Thus, we cannot separate the person from community, s/he is always a person-in-community, rooted in an ongoing ever-developing tradition shaped and reshaped in critical thought and social practice. Therefore, the collective and personal exist in the social context in a reciprocal unity, and we temporarily use separate categories below only to view them with more analytical preciseness.

Maatian ethics begin and develop in a concern for the quality of human relations and the respect for the human personality and community this requires. It is a fundamental African ethical principle that the human being realizes him or herself only in moral relations with others. The basis of fundamental concern, then, is never the isolated individual but the related person, the person-in-community (1). When Kheti teaches that humans are in the image of God, he does it in the collective not in the singular (2) (Husia:52). Moreover, he makes the Divine legacy a collective legacy. The legacy is one of the heavens and earth, life, a nature in God's image, nourishment from nature, security and care, righteous rulers and "leaders that lift the load from the back of the weak," and finally, "words of power as a weapon to ward off the blow of evil events." This attribution of divinity to the human personality carries within it an obligation to act a certain way towards oneself as well as toward one's fellow humans, i.e., with ultimate respect for the worth and dignity of the human personality. Also one is obligated to emulate God in terms of His qualities and acts of beneficence, generosity and mercy towards humans. Thus, the theology and ethics in the Declarations of Innocence and Virtue reflect these obligations. And one is also obligated, as the texts teach, to preserve and share the legacy and pass it on to future generations.

It is important to note here that although the Declarations of Innocence are stated in the negative as to what was not done wrong, they represent, as I have stated above, "What one should be able to say" to justify and vindicate oneself morally before history and heaven. They are a body of moral obligations accepted by the ancient Egyptians, as well as standards of right and wrong and ethical ideals for the conduct and development of one's life. Therefore, I will discuss them as such and try to recover and reconstruct the valuable legacy they offer.

A. Obligations to Others

The first two obligations in the Declarations of Innocence are not to mistreat fellow human beings. The first is not to mistreat people in general and implicitly those you don't know. The second is not to mistreat or rather not to impoverish familiars. The first obligation is literally not to do wrong or isfet to people as people (remetchet). It is again a reflection of the Maatian stress on respect for the divinity in the human personality and his/her worth and dignity as a fellow human being. In fact, in the Ikeru (Declarations of Virtue), we read of Paheri's declaration that "I know the God that dwells in man and woman. And knowing him I knew this from that [i.e., right from wrong] and performed the tasks..." accordingly (Husia:94). Knowing the divinity of the human person, Paheri acted toward them accordingly, never confusing the messenger with the message, never speaking vulgar words and always being the "model of kindness".

The second obligation is not to impoverish your family and friends, literally your familiars. The word used is "wendjut" which does not simply mean associates as Faulkner (3) cites, but also familiars, one's circle of significant others, i.e., family, friends, neighbors, etc. But it could by extension also mean fellow human beings in a more intimate way than "remetchet". Thus, wendjut are the human others so essential to moral conception and conduct. These are one's measure and mirror in both the moral and social sense. They are the "neighbor" you should not bear false witness against in Jewish and Christian ethics, "the brother and sister of faith" to whom you are obligated in Islamic ethics, and the fellow human you must recognize and respect in Confucian and Hindu ethics.

The value of the category is that it allows for both an intimate and general definition of others, i.e., family and friends or neighbor and fellow human. In the Husia (109), I translated wendjut to mean "family and associates" but it could just as well been translated by other words. In fact, various authors have translated it in various ways. For example, Rossiter translated it as "kindred" (4); Allen as "people" (5); Faulkner as "associates" (6); and Budge as "members of my family" (7).

Another interesting concept in the declaration is that of not impoverishing one's familiars. It is worth reflection to consider how one might impoverish one's fellow or familiar. The word is "semar" meaning impoverish or make wretched. It is a challenging concept, one which taken in the positive means we are obligated or at least should strive to enrich our relationships with others. This at a minimum means always adding something new and positive to them and always being concerned with maintaining and practicing reciprocity. On the other hand, it means at least to keep what is good and do not lose anything of value you share in the relationship.

It is important to note here that some authors have wondered why the Declarations make no mention of family relations. But this category, wendjut, might have been inclusive of relations with family as argued above. Certainly, family relations were key in both the Ikeru and the Sebait and one could legitimately expect them in the Declarations. Thus, the reference to wendjut might have seemed sufficient. Moreover, as Petrie notes, "It would be quite possible that in a matriarchal society, the permanent bond of family was not looked on as entailing duties different in kind than those equally due to relatives and neighbors in general" [8]. Again, "wendjut" appears relevant here and accepting Petrie's stress on what is more correctly called the "matri-focal" character of the African or Egyptian family, one could see how the ethic of care and responsibility would be more generalized. Thus, the community would become a kind of extended family and the naturalness of the relations would not seem to necessitate direct and singular mention of one's family as distinct from other familiars.

Moreover, Petrie states, "in the historical ages of the Vth and XIXth Dynasties, the family duties are far more lightly touched on than we would expect and there is none of that clannish sense of solidarity which is the basis of society to western peoples." Thus, he concludes, the absence of stress on particular family duties may suggest a broad sense of fellow human obligation and sensitivity. And in such a case, "the absence of certain classes of feelings and ideas may often show more than the presence of particular injuctions." Finally, it is important to note that the Sebait and Ikeru are full of obligations to one's family and thus, there is no neglect in Maatian ethical literature of this obligation. But in the Declarations a broader sense of human obligation is suggested and affirmed.

There are several categories of offenses one should avoid committing in showing due respect for fellow humans. They can be classified for the sake of discussion into obligations against violence, other injuries, deprivations and deceptions. Naturally, any serious ethics must deal with prohibitions against taking human life, which shows the ultimate disrespect of the human person. This injuction against killing is also written in the Sebait in which Kheti says, "Do not kill, for it will not profit you" (Husia:51). The implication here is that not only is the sanctity of life violated but the moral community is degraded and diminished. There is in the Declarations not only an injuction against killing but also commanding another to kill. Thus, one does not escape moral responsibility by having another do one's dirty work. One is responsible, then, not only for what one does directly, but also for what one contributes to indirectly.

One is also obligated not to terrorized or rob anyone which are other forms of violence. This is stressed in the teachings of Ptah-Hotep who says, "Do not terrorize people for if you do, God will punish you accordingly." The law of reciprocity, he teaches, insures that what is done to others will be done to you; thus, he says the robber will end up being robbed and the conspirator entrapped by his/her own means. Therefore, he teaches, "one should live in peace with others" and they will willingly share what the violent person would try to coerce from them.

Injunctions against causing pain, suffering, hunger and even making another cry also appear in the Declarations. These injuries, like violence represent inadequate respect for the human person and implicitly cultivate the grounds for erosion and undermining of moral community. Thus, one must not only be innocent of large offenses [causing hunger, pain, suffering] but also sensitive enough to avoid what seems to be small offenses [making another cry], for each represents damage to the social and moral fabric of community. Thus, one should always do what strengthens community, friendship and fellow human sensitivity and then one can always draw from the rich treasure of positive and reciprocal relations. As Phebhor teaches, "Those who love their neighbors will [always] find a family around them" [Husia:69].

The obligations not to injure persons by violating their personal and family relations and space are also important. Therefore, gossiping, slander, and eavesdropping are prohibitied in the Declarations. Speech is both a special human gift and power but it can also be used as a weapon to destroy reputations, undermine trust among people, misinform and mislead. Thus, the Declarations teach restraint on the tongue, i.e., one should not lie, curse, engage in quarrelling, slander, be overly talkative or loud of voice. Likewise, the Sebait also teach against injurious speech, "One should not injure others with your tongue," Amenomope advises us [Husia:61]. Moreover, Ani teaches that even as gossip hurts others, it can also hurt you by backfiring on you. Thus, he admonishes, "Never speak evil words to any [one]; a word spoken carelessly some day when you are gossiping may overturn your house" [Husia:55]. In a word, "a person can be ruined by his/her tongue" [Husia:56]. And Ankhsheshonqi teaches that "If a man and woman are at peace with each other, they will never fare badly, but if they gossip about each other, they will never fare well" [Husia:65].

Sexual morality is also important in the Declarations of Innocence. The stress is on restraint and responsibility; thus, there are prohibitions against perversity, unchastness and adultery. The first degrades the human person, the second implies violations of personal and social standards of discipline and the third, violation of one of the most important relations in community. Phebhor teaches that control of sexual appetite is key to character and reputation. And Ptah-Hotep teaches that friendship, peace, family stability and personal and community prosperity depend on responsible sexual relations. Thus, he says, "If you want friendship to last in the house you enter as master, friend or brother, or in any other place you enter, avoid approaching the women in an improper manner. No place is peaceful where this is done and he who intrudes on them is unwelcome. Thousands of men have been ruined for the pleasure of a short moment, which passes like a dream and then brings death to those who have indulged in it. Men and women leave home because of it and the heart should refrain from it. As for those who go wrong because of lust, none of their plans will prosper" [Husia:44].

The Declarations also express an obligation not to deprive others of what is theirs and what is due. This includes prohibitions against stealing food and property, encroaching on other's fields, lessening the acre, taking from the orphan, discrimination, and tampering with the scales. All this point to the moral issue of social justice. Maat above all is truth, justice and righteousness. Justice, then, stands at the heart of what it means to follow Maat and create a Maatian moral community. And justice begins with respecting the human person and giving her [him] her [his] due. In African ethics, shared social wealth is essential. This is why even in a class society, it is ethically compelling to share wealth with the poor and vulnerable. Thus, Maatian ethics in the Virtues and Declarations obligate each to "give food to the hungry, water to the thirsty, clothes to the naked and a boat to those without one." The ultimate ethical challenge is to end poverty itself, but active moral sensitivity to the poor and an obligation to aid them are beginning steps.

Wealth in Kemetic society was seen as a gift from God to aid others. As Phebhor teaches, "God allows one to acquire wealth in return for doing good." Also, "wealth goes to those who give food to others by means of it." Therefore, he says, "if you acquire property, give a portion to God by giving a portion to the poor" [Husia:69].

Ptah-Hotep teaches one should "be generous as long as you live. What goes into the storehouse should come out. For bread is made to be shared" [Husia:47]. And Ankhsheshonqi teaches, "let your generosity reach one who needs it. Do not be stingy, for wealth is no real security." And finally, speaking to the role of reciprocity in a moral community, Ani says, "If you are found generous in times of prosperity, when adversity comes you will be able to bear it" [Husia:55]. For, of course, your friends and neighbors will share with you as you have shared with them. Thus, as Ptah-Hotep teaches, "it is not food or wealth which sustains a people and community; it is righteousness" [Husia:45].

The point here is that the Declarations reaffirm a fundamental theme in Kemetic ethics, social justice and within this, a special concern, an ethics of care and responsibility for the vulnerable. Thus, the orphan, widow, elderly, diasbled, and the small child are focuses of special concern, and generosity is a much-stressed personal and social virtue. Likewise, greed and covetousness are condemned throughout the ethical literature. It is important to stress that Maatian ethics stands on the side of the poor and vulnerable and that implicit in this stand is the concept that the quality of life and justice in any society is measured by how it treats its most vulnerable members. Thus, again and again in the literature, discrimination is condemned and equal justice and respect for rich and poor, humble and great, unlearned and wise are taught as the ethical ideal. Even the stranger is to be shown moral concern and shared with equitably. Thus, Amenomope says, "Do not refuse your oil jar to a stranger to double it for your family and friends. God loves those who respect the poor more than those who revere the rich" (Husia:63). And even if we concede that practice didn't and doesn't always coincide with principle, the existence of the standard is itself an indispensible beginning and inspiration to strive for and achieve the ideal. And this, of course, has been and remains a central historical human project, i.e., the quest for a truly just and good society.

Linked to this concern for justice is the obligation in the Declarations to avoid deception, lying, cheating and fraud. "Speak the truth to everyone. Let it cling to your speech," Ankhsheshonqi teaches (Husia:66). And Amenomope teaches that speaking falsely and being deceptive is a moral abomination. "Do not mislead man or woman with pen and papyrus. Do not bear witness with false words nor injure another with your tongue." Also, he teaches against fraud with pen and taxing the poor. He advises truth and justice and says, "You will find this a path of life. You will pass the night in sound sleep and in the morning find it again like good news." For, he says, "Better is praise with the love of others than wealth in the storehouse" (Husia:61).

Much stress is also placed on economic justice in Maatian ethics and obligations against fraud, especially against the vulnerable. Therefore, the Declarations stress honest and fair business ethics as well as economic justice in the general sense. One is not to encroach on others' fields, add or take from the weight of the scales, tamper with the tongue of the scales, or take milk from mouths of children. Likewise, in the Sebait, one is commanded to forgive debts of the poor and not tax them when they have nothing, and not to gain riches by robbery. Moreover, in all things justice should be done for the poor and the prosperous, the weak as well as the strong. For justice, says Amenomope, is a divine gift and "Surely the strength of one who is like God saves the wretched from the oppressor" [Husia:62].

B. Personal Obligations

Maatian ethics is a virtue ethics, that is to say an ethics concerned with building moral character and a moral community which sustains and is sutained by such charactrer. Maatian ethics posits the model person as the geru-maa, the truly self-mastered person "whose whole character is infused with Maat". The word is made up of "geru" which means silent, self-controlled, self-mastered and "maa" which means truly or righteous. Thus, geru-maa means the truly self-mastered. It is Amenomope who defines the geru-maa as one who sets him/herself apart, and is "like a tree grown in fertile ground," doubly productive and beneficial to all around [Husia:59].

The Declarations impose obligations of righteous thought, emotion, speech and conduct so that the Maatian person is cultivated through the development of character. And character is developed through moral instruction and practice. Thus, in Maatian ethics, instruction and learning are above all for a practical end, self-cultivation-in-community. As Ankhsheshonqi says, "It is in the development of character that instruction succeeds." Therefore, one is cultivated to do good and abstain from evil. In the Declarations one is obligated: not to be arrogant, covetous, greedy, or quick-tempered, in order to cultivate the mind and emotions; not to lie, curse, argue, engage in quarrelling or be contentious, gossip, slander or talk overmuch, in order to cultivate restraint in speech; and not to demand more than what is due to one, mistreat others, kill, bring forth one's name for praise, be deceitful, cheat, steal, commit sexually harmful acts, stir-up strife, terrorize, use violence or be aggressive, in order to cultivate moral conduct.

Then, one is cultivated to do good by instruction in the seven cardinal virtues of Maat: truth, justice, propriety, harmony, balance, reciprocity and order. These are cardinal in that all of these categories can be and are translated in the sacred texts as Maat. Thus, to speak truth, do justice, act properly, live in harmony, be balanced, practice reciprocity and recognize and respect the personal-social, divine and natural order are all Maat. The thrust to cultivate the Maatian character is to create a self-enriching process in which the Maatian person and Maatian society, in a dynamic reciprocity, reinforce and sustain each other and foster each other's expansiveness.

III. Obligations to the Divine

The Declarations of Innocence's concern with ethics toward the Divine is essentially directed toward due respect for God and sacred property and ritual. Therefore, there are prohibitions against blasphemy against God and cursing his representative on earth, the King or Queen. The latter is due to the divine conception of kingship and the Kemetic social order. It was seen not as simply a social realm, but an extension and reflection of the Divine. Thus, it too was sacred and acts against it were grave offenses. Likewise, acts against the Temples called "peru-netcher", House of God, and its property were seen as serious violations.

But the real obligations to God like the real obligations to family are implicit in the obligations to other humans. In fact, as Phebhor says, what you wish to do for God, do for others, especially the most vulnerable. "The heart of God is satisfied when the poor stand provided for before Him. Thus, if you acquire property, give a portion to God, by giving a portion to the poor" (Husia:69). Wealth is given by God so that one can do good, he contends, "And those who give food to the poor God takes them to himself in mercy without measure." This also is Amenomope's position when he teaches that "Justice is a gift of God. . .and the strength of one who is like God saves the wretched from their oppressor.

Here we return to the two obligations mentioned above which flow from attribution of divine nature to humans. Maatian anthropology and ethics pose humans in the image of God and place on them obligations to act as such on both the social and personal level. They must, then, act always to respect the worth and dignity of the human person in terms of themselves and others. And they must imitate Ra, God in his infinite Goodness. The spiritual and ethical portrait of God is one who hates evil and loves Good, even in the most ancient texts, i.e., the Shabaka Text and the Pyramid Texts, in the Book of Prayers and Sacred Praises (Husia:13ff). He is revealed as "protector of the humble and the needy, merciful, forgiving, the prime minister of the poor, the truly just judge, a father and mother to the orphan, a husband to the widow, liberator of captives, creator, Bringer-into-Being, beneficent of heart, doctor and healer, a gentle God with effective counsel." This, then, is the real ethical and spiritual challenge of Maatian theology and ethics in terms of obligations to the Divine, to honor the image we claim by imitating the righteousness claimed for the God in whose image we say we are. This in the final analysis, means commitment in thought, emotion and practice to a just and good society in which the image and interest of humans are respected in the ultimate sense and an ethic of care and responsibility is pervasive and natural.

IV. Obligations to Nature

The natural ethical concerns of Maatian ethics flow from the concept of a holistic universe, an order founded on and sustained by Maat. As other Africans, ancient Egyptians had the highest respect for nature and felt and expressed a kinship with it. To the ancient Egyptian, Maat was the unifying principle that bound all together, from the universe to humans, to the fish in the sea and the chick in the egg, as Akhnaton's Great Hymn to Aten [Ra] so poetically expresses. It is only natural and logical, then, that Maatian ethics would include obligations toward nature.

Kheti's paean to Ra, quoted above, lays the theological and ethical basis for respect for nature [Husia:52]. He poses the world as a heritage and legacy given by God for humans for nourishment, sustainability and enjoyment. He implies trusteeship or stewardship as an obligatory role for humans. This means an ethic of care and responsibility in the natural realm similar to the one we practice in the social realm. This would and does include, at a minimum, according to the sacred texts, preservation and sharing of the environment, humane ethical treatment of animals, and an implied obligation to pass on the legacy and the obligation to preserve it to future generations.

In the Declarations of Innocence we read that one is obligated not to wade in or pollute water, stop it when it should flow or dam it so that it blocks others' equal access to it. One must, likewise, not put out fire when it should burn. For even this is guided by the principle of shared environment and benefits of the earth. Humane treatment of animals has been a long and emphasized ethical obligation of ancient Egyptians. As early as the Pyramid Texts, we discover that part of the righteousness the departed kings claimed was not having mistreated even animals. In Unas' Pyramid Text, we read: "No one alive accuses Unas. No dead accuses Unas.

No goose [or] ox accuses Unas" [10]. Thus, Lichtheim is correct to interpret this as a declaration of moral purity which asserts that Unas "has done no wrong to man, bird or beast."

Also, Piankhi's Victory Text likewise shows a strong sensitivity to care for animals and Breasted reports in Ancient Records a Declaration of Virtue which shows a nomarch reporting that in times of famine, he fed not only the human hungry but even the wolves of the mountain area. The principle here appears to be one of avoiding behavior, even toward animals, that would diminish or damage the humanity of the person him/herself. The stress, then, is on respect for nature and its various parts - land and water, birds and animals, for several reasons: 1) because it's an ethical obligation to preserve the world entrusted to us; 2) because damage to it or its parts damages us in some important way; and 3) because to damage nature is not only to deprive ourselves of a sustainable environment, but also deprive future generations of one.

The world, as a common ecological environment, is currently under several kinds of pressure, including the problems of pollution of air, water and soil, and depletion of other natural resources. The threats to the environment not only affect the possibilities of future generations, but the very existence of the world as we know it. Clearly, an ethics that links life in a holistic framework and makes it morally compelling to respect both the social and the natural is needed. Maatian ethics stresses such a holistic approach, positing an indestructible unity of the human, Divine and natural. It is, even in its ancient form, committed to a just, good and righteous order in the social and natural realm. From this, one can evolve a social and environmental ethics which are interrelated and interdependent. In fact, the obligation to preserve the environment for ourselves and future generations derives from the same ethics to preserve and promote human life and development. For it compels us not to do anything which would deny or diminish the chances for a full and fulfilling life for each and every person.

It is thus unethical in a Maatian sense, to destroy or damage nature, for it eliminates or diminishes chances for a full and fulfilling human life. Moreover, it violates a trust posed in Kheti's concept of responsible trusteeship. Therefore, when we pollute the seas with waste and oil spillage, destroy wilderness areas and rain forests for profit, poison air and water, we violate a divine and human trust. It violates also the obligation posed in the Declaration of Innocence not to be arrogant and assume the earth exists simply for our utility for the moment with no thought of what it means to animal and plant life or future generations. This is anthropocentricism at its worse, a self-centeredness that is not only detrimental to nature, but in the end, also to the reckless, destructive and uncaring person which it creates.

This is not an animal and nature rights argument that equates human rights with animal interests or nature's claims on our respect. But it is an ethics which sees a vital relationship between nature and humans that requires the respect for both and rejects thoughtless, uncaring and irresponsible behavior which threatens both human life and the environment. The need, then, is again for an ethics of care and responsibility which recognizes the limits of nature, and the obligation to share it responsibly with others and refuses to exploit it for superficial wants of consumerism while other human beings lack vital necessities. Moreover, such an ethics refuses to use the earth as if it were private property rather than a truly human heritage to be shared through just distribution and responsible use of resources.

Finally, our ethic of care and responsibility toward nature requires us to preserve nature for future generations. Our posterity has a right to see whales and elephants alive rather than in films and photos, to drink clean water and breathe unpolluted air and enjoy beaches unmarred by waste. And to pollute and poison the earth, air and water, to deplete nonrenewable resources of the planet is to erode the quality of human life for the future and thus violate the rights of future generations. Likewise, the nuclear and industrial technology which threaten the earth also threaten future generations as well as those living now. Here the virtue of justice is required also for nature, ourselves and others, including future generations. Also needed is the virtue of service to others [wenut] which in turn benefits us and builds and reinforces moral community. It is morally unjustifiable to disregard the predictable effects of irresponsible and uncaring behavior towards the environment on future generations. The very existence of future generations depends on the ethical character and behavior of persons alive now. It is, thus, morally compelling that we strive to limit damage to the earth, curtail and end wasteful consumerism, and respect the claims of nature - animate and inanimate - on us. As the ancient Egyptians taught, if we wish to live for eternity, we must build for eternity. And as Seba Kheti taught, "Everyday is a donation to eternity and even one hour is a contribution to the future."

Notes

1. John Mbiti. African Religions and Philosophy, Garden City,NY: Anchor Books, 1970.

2. Since most of the quotations in this chapter will be from the Husia, I will cite the reference inside the text for convenience of author and reader.

3. Raymond O. Faulkner. A Concise Dictionary of Middle Egyptian, Oxford: Griffith Institute, 1981.

4. Evelyn Rossiter. The Book of the Dead, Geneva: Productions Libre, 1979, p. 91.

5. Thomas Allen. The Book of the Dead, Chicago: University of Chicago Press, 1974, p. 97.

6. R. O. Faulkner. The Book of the Dead, London: British Museum Publications, 1985. p. 29.

7. E.A. Wallis Budge. The Book of the Dead, Volume II, London: Kegan, Paul Trench, p. 191.

8. W.F. Petrie. Religion and Conscience in Ancient Egypt, London: Methune & Co., 1948, p. 146, 147.

9. Siegfried Morenz. Egyptian Religion, Ithaca, NY:Cornell University Press, 1978, p. 118.

10. Miriam Lichtheim. Ancient Egyptian Literature, Volume I, Los Angeles: University of California Press, 1975, p. 35.

SECTION IV - REFERENCES

BIBLIOGRAPHY

Ancient Egyptian Religion, Mythology and Ethics

Breasted, James. Development of Religion and Thought in Ancient Egypt, Philadelphia: University of Pennsylvania Press, 1986.

Breasted, James. The Dawn of Conscience, New York: Charles Scribner's, 1934.

Budge, E.A. Wallis. From Fetish to God in Ancient Egypt, London: Oxford University Press, 1934.

Budge, E.A. Wallis. The Gods of the Egyptians or Studies in Egyptian Mythology, New York: Dover Publications, 1969.

Budge, E.A. Wallis. Osiris and the Egyptian Resurrection, New York: Dover Publications, 1968.

Cerny, Jaroslav. Ancient Egyptian Religion, London: Hutchinson, 1952.

Clark, Rundle T. Myth and Symbol in Ancient Egypt, London: Thames & Hudson, 1959.

David, Rosalie. Cult of the Sun: Myth and Magic in Ancient Egypt, Toronto: J.M. Dent & Sons, 1980.

Erman, Adolf. A Handbook of Egyptian Religion, London: Constable, 1907.

Frankfort, Henri. Ancient Egyptian Religion: An Interpretation, New York: Harper & Row, 1961

Frankfort, Henri. Kingship and the Gods, Chicago: University of Chicago Press, 1969.

Griffiths, J.G. The Conflict of Horus and Seth, Liverpool: The University Press, 1960.

Hart, George. A Dictionary of Egyptian Gods and Goddesses, London: Routledge and Kegan Paul, 1986.

Hoffneier, James K. Sacred in the Vocabulary of Ancient Egypt, Fribourg, Switzerland: Univer-saitatsverlag, 1985.

Hornung, Erik. Conceptions of God in Ancient Egypt, Ithaca, NY: Cornell University Press, 1982.

Ions, Veronia. Egyptian Mythology, London: Hamlyn, 1965.

Karenga, Maulana. The Book of Coming Forth By Day: The Ethics of the Declarations of Innocence, Los Angeles: University of Sankore Press, 1990.

Karenga, Maulana. Selections from the Husia: Sacred Wisdom of Ancient Egypt, Los Angeles: Unversity of Sankore Press, 1984.

Karenga, Maulana. "Towards a Sociology of Maatian Ethics: Literature and Context," in Maulana Karenga (ed.) Reconstructing Kemetic Culture, Los Angeles: University of Sankore Press, 1990, pp. 66-96.

Lurker, Manfred. The Gods and Symbols of Ancient Egypt, London: Thames & Hudson, 1980.

Mercer, Samuel. The Religion of Ancient Egypt, London: Luzac & Co., Ltd., 1949.

Mercetante, A.S. Who's Who in Egyptian Mythology, New York: C. Potter, 1978.

Morenz, Siegfried, Egyptian Religion, Ithaca, New York: Cornell University Press, 1978.

Petrie, W.M. Flinders. Religion and Conscience in Ancient Egypt, London: Methuen & Co., 1898.

Renouf, P. Le Page. The Hibbert Lectures: Lectures on the Origin and Growth of Religion as Illustrated by the Religion of Ancient Egypt, London: Williams and Norgate, 1897.

Remond, E.A.E. The Mythical Origin of the Egyptian Temple, New York: Barnes and Noble, 1969.

Sauneron, Serge. The Priests of Ancient Egypt, New York: Grove Press, 1969.

Shorter, Alan. The Egyptian Gods: A Handbook, New York: Macmillan, 1937.

Shorter, A. W. An Introduction to Egyptian Religion, London: K. Paul, Trench, Trubner & Co., 1931.

Wainwright, G.A. The Sky-Religion in Egypt, Westport, CT: Greenwood, 1938.

Zabkar, L.V. A Study of the Ba Concept in Ancient Egyptian Texts, Chicago: Oriental Institute Press, 1968.